BLACK SURVIVAL *IN*
WHITE AMERICA:

BLACK

SURVIVAL *IN*

WHITE

AMERICA:

From Past History to the Next Century

By **Jeanette Davis-Adeshote'**

BRYANT AND DILLON PUBLISHERS, INC.
ORANGE, NEW JERSEY

Cover Design Laurie Williams / A Street Called Straight

Photograph Courtesy of T & F Camera, Vineland, N.J.

Edited by Gwendolynne A. Blakeley

Requests for permission to make copies of any part of the work should be mailed to: Permissions Department,
BRYANT AND DILLON PUBLISHERS, INC.
P.O. Box-39, Orange, New Jersey 07050

Library of Congress Cataloging in Publication Data
Davis-Adeshote', Jeanette
1. Black Survival in White America   2. History 3. Current Affairs
(A BRYANT AND DILLON BOOK)

CIP# 94-79897
ISBN 0-9638672-3-7

Printed in the United States of America
10 9 8 7 6 5 4 3 2 1

This Book is Dedicated to:

My Mother, **Isabella Beverly-Ashby**; Son, **Darryl**; Sister, **Gloria Lynn**; Brothers, **Nat**, **Leon**, **Forrest**; the spirit of my deceased brother, **Ernest** and the entire Beverly Family who are legion.

Special Thanks to **Dr. Maya Angelou** for the gift of her poem, "Black Family Pledge".

Special thanks to my cousin **Joyce Beverly** for being there when I needed you, and my Supervisor, **George Diament** for being understanding while writing was in progress. Last, but not least, thanks to **Emile, Gerri and James** for your guidance, support and belief in this endeavor.

Table of Contents

BLACK FAMILY PLEDGE

Because we have forgotten our ancestors, our children no longer give us honor.

Because we have lost the path our ancestors cleared kneeling in perilous undergrowth, our children cannot find their way.

Because we have banished the God of our ancestors, our children cannot pray.

Because the old ways of our ancestors have faded beyond our hearing our children cannot hear us crying.

Because we have abandoned our wisdom of mothering and fathering, our befuddled children give birth to children they neither want nor understand.

Because we have forgotten how to love, the adversary is within our gates and holds us up to the mirror of the world, shouting, "Regard the loveless."

Therefore, we pledge to bind ourselves to one another.

To embrace our lowest.

To keep company with our loneliest.

To educate our illiterate.

To feed our starving.

To clothe our ragged.

To do all good things, knowing that we are more than keepers of our brothers and sisters. We are our brothers and sisters.

In honor of those who toiled and implored God with golden tongues, and gratitude to the same God who brought us out of hopeless desolation,

WE MAKE THIS PLEDGE.

Dr. Maya Angelou.

I

SELF IDENTITY

W ho am I? Where did I come from? Why am I subjected to hatred because of the color of my skin and Africoid characteristics? Why do I hate my blackness? Why do white people think they are superior to me? These questions plague today's black youth, and a large number of black adults in America. Answers resound from many quarters seeking to quell inner rage festering within the breasts of a people long tired of being tired. But should the rage be postponed one more time? Should the fires within be once more doused with promises of renewal, or should a new attitude, a different perspective, take shape? Superficial band-aiding has proven futile, for setbacks have catapulted people of magnificent hues from upward mobility toward downward slides reminiscent of the 1950's. It is past time for these questions to be answered and long-time solutions suggested.

The beginning of a new perspective should start with awareness of the Africoid physical characteristics found in black people.

Physical characteristics should be unimportant, but since they are the most distinguishing factors used in discrimination, black children should understand why they look the way they do and the purposes for their wide noses, extra curly hair, large lips, protruding buttocks and dark pigments.

The wide nose of African people creates a quality of tone unlike any in the world. The nose, mouth, throat and chest work together to create a rich tone in speaking and singing. These organs show complete evolved capacity.[1]

The hair of African people is designed by nature for maximum protection of the brain. The skull is thicker because we have completely evolved (Dawn Man or Australopithecus fled Africa and migrated to Europe before completely evolving, thus the slim nose and stringy hair was retained). The wavy pattern of the hair has bounce to minimize damage to the skull and brain when coming into contact with objects in the environment. Blacks changing the quality of their hair (straighteners), lessens nature's protection.[2]

Apes have thin lips like the European migrating Australopithecus. The African feature of full lips indicate readiness of sexual desire. The fuller the lips, the more readiness. This has been an evolving characteristic throughout the ages. White females, in efforts to make their lips seem fuller and swelled with sexual desire, color outside of their natural lip lines. Today, they use collagen to bring their lips, that are inside of their mouths, outside of their mouths (this indicates the lack of evolving fully).[3]

"The Gluteous Maximus was not only a survival development when he (the African) was hunted, but also for maneuverability when hunting. The buttock muscle's development is in direct proportion to both running speed, jumping and maneuverability. It is most highly developed in the Africans."[4]

Melanin causes skin color. "It is a brown liquid chemical secreted from cells located in the epidermis of the skin giving color and protection to the skin."[5] "It protects against aging, harmful radiations (like those emitted from the sun), air-borne abrasives, long immersion in water, and harmful effects of cold. It also aids in speedier muscular responses, better sight and increases the sensing of "vibes" in the environment."[6] Melanin is also found in everyone's brain, eyes and nervous system. It is so useful to the body, that scientists are perplexed by its functions all of which have not yet been determined.

All of these qualities come with being of recent African descent. (All people are of African descent, but changed do to climatic conditions in new locations during migratory periods in the past). Because of these physical possessions, African people have been able to sustain untold hardship, and still exist today to bleach and straighten that that has sustained them. Children should be taught to be proud of how they look naturally, and who they are. There is no benefit in imitating those wishing to have their African lips and skin. No one upon the earth has hair like them. The closest thing to it is lamb's wool. Oh yes, Jesus had hair of lamb's wool, didn't he?

It is insanity to think white people hate black people. They admire black beauty. They tan themselves to obtain color. Many inject their lips to look sexy. Some even have surgery on their buttocks to extend them. They admire the rhythmic way black people dance and sing because they lack this natural ability. The strength and spirituality of Blacks never ceases to amaze Whites who tend to admire Blacks more than hate them. The tendency is to envy physical and inner qualities of people of color and want it for themselves.

The white power structure has economic control, but now wants control over nature's biological network. Their reaction is childlike when science fails. They develop a certain disdain for those who possess what they want. However great a challenge this may present, do not believe any one of them would exchange hues with anyone of color if it meant giving up power.

The society in which we live not only plays games with physical makeup, it also plays games in the marketplace. With majority individuals, everything boils down to economics. With every generation, a new game is played, or rules change keeping Blacks and other minorities outside the arena.

During the 1960's great civil battles were fought, out of which came the Civil Rights Bill. In the 1990's black youth were sent off to battle Arabs, while the President determined a Civil Rights Bill inadequate. Blacks fought well for equality, but sat down too soon to enjoy a victory not yet won. What do they say to their youth searching for answers? How do they now give them hope if their hopes have waned? Survival belongs to the wise as well as the strong. It is time to teach black youth that which breeds hope, instills pride, and creates determination that will not tolerate defeat, nor weaken in time.

Youth seeks and probes for answers. That is their nature. They're seeking foremost, identity. Who am I? It's a complex question during puberty. Disintegration of their personalities due to hormonal changes is a biological certainty. Black youth have an added dimension in searching for that identity, because they live in a society that resents their presence and fears them, especially black males. It has become increasingly impossible for some black youth to realize enjoyments of adolescence experienced by majority youth, because of environmental factors. Their development is tarnished and hastened by early encounters with criminal elements within their communities, black-on-black destruction due to self-hate, and surviving on the dregs of society. This has hardened them and stolen their youthful innocence. All black youth, at some point in their early development, are exposed to racism in its ugliest forms. What does this say to them? It serves as a mirror reflecting back what is hated; the color of their skin. At such an impressionable age, when personality structure is taking shape, they absorb the hatred of self into self. "I am hated because I am ugly. I am ugly because I am black." They do not know where to go from here. Had they been given tools to deal with such confrontations earlier in life, they would have been better prepared to resist such notions. The parents of today's youth experienced devastating self-hate programming during their early development also.

When the miracle of television arrived in the late 1940's, Blacks were prime targets without realizing it. Cowboy shows with the good guys dressed in white (especially white hats), and the bad guys dressed in black, had fist fights. The hats never came off, especially during fight scenes and the good guys always won.

And what about the commercials with cars racing down the highway demonstrating the one with the best gasoline? The black one always came up short. The monsters were black, Daffy Duck (who never won) was black, anything relating to the macabre was black, and all dialogue dealing with negativity was described as black.

The message was loud and clear. Black was negative, bad, ugly, unneeded, disliked and unwanted in a predominately pristine "white" society. Inwardly, black children began to feel unneeded, disliked and unwanted at an early age. It didn't take long for them to hear it spoken, for they grew up fighting inequities and taunts of "nigger". Knowing all this, why haven't black tactics changed? Why are Blacks fighting old battles with archaic weapons? A change is in the wind, and youth leads the charge. Let us look at the messages they are sending.

The youth of today are casting their collective fate to the wind. Their dress, hair styles, demeanor, rap and communication with each other and the world, wreaks of freedom. They cover their pain with bravado. Only mature Blacks see the pain and hurt in their actions, words and eyes. Their hair, ornaments, dress and kente cloths scream "Africa". They look beyond the older generation to a far off place to reclaim themselves. They look for a beauty they can spread, and have been spreading all over America through their music and style. They've done a pretty good job for now pale lips are being injected with collagen (appreciation for that which was deemed ugly). A small victory, but a victory nonetheless. These youth are bombarding America with arrogant pride, and she doesn't know what to make of it. Is it real self love being exhibited, or pain in disguise? Some brothers and sisters would venture to say, "Whatever it is, it's good, so let it be." It is beneficial in some ways. It's good because it instills pride and a direction for youngsters hearing about who they are for the first time, but more needs to be done by parents and educators. Black youth need to know the beauty of self from an ancient perspective. The stories of their people's gifts to humanity reign supreme in the history of the world, but they are not privy to that history through the usual avenues of home, society and academia. Read, *"Africa, Mother of Western Civilization"* by Yosef ben-Jochanan. They need to know about principles laid down by their forefathers for their longevity and peaceful living.

One of the world's first religions, MAAT, the divine principle of Truth, Justice and Righteousness, laid the foundation for social order, natural order and unity within ancient Nubian (black African) Egyptian society. These ancestors of black people today, practiced these principles 2,000 years before the Ten Commandments came into existence. (Read, *"African Origin of the Major Western Religions"* by Yosef ben-Jochanan).

These principles are:

"I have not done iniquity. I have not robbed with violence. I have not stolen. I have not made any to suffer pain. I have not defrauded offerings. I have done no murder nor bid anyone to slay on my behalf. I have not trimmed the measure. I have not spoken lies. I have not robbed God. I have not caused the shedding of tears. I have not dealt deceitfully. I have not acted guilefully. I have not laid waste to the land. I have not set my lips against anyone. I have not been angry or wrathful without just cause. I have not lusted nor defiled the wife of any man. I have not polluted myself. I have not caused terror. I have not done that which is abominable. I have not multiplied words exceedingly. I have never uttered fiery words. I have not judged hastily. I have not transgressed nor have I vexed or angered God. I have not stopped my ears against the words of Right and Truth. I have not burned with rage. I have not worked grief. I have not acted with insolence. I have not avenged myself. I have not stirred up strife. I have not been an eavesdropper. I have not wronged the people. I have done no harm nor have I done evil. I have not worked treason. I have never fouled the water. I have not spoken scornfully. I have never cursed God. I have not behaved with arrogance. I have not envied or craved for that which belongs to another. I have not filched food from the mouth of the infant. I have done no hurt unto man, nor wrough harm unto beasts. I have never magnified my condition beyond what was fitting."

Ptah-hotep stated in 2370 B.C., "Let your life be an example and live justly, for if justice remains a firm foundation, your children will prosper." For more information, read, *"MAAT: The African Universe"*, by Jacob H. Carruthers. Also informative reading would be, *"Ancient Egyptian Religions"*, by Henri Frankfort. The foundation for living full, fruitful lives laid down by our ancestors has been lost, hidden, and now reclaimed for our renewal. The greatness of ancestors long unknown to our people, must now be revealed to black youth to instill pride, awareness of the greatness lying dormant within them, and awaken high self-esteem so dearly lacking today. Read, *"Origin of the Ancient Egyptians"* by Cheikh Anta Diop and *"Black Rulers of the Golden Age"* by Legrand H. Clegg II.

Blacks are spiritual people, and with religion being an important part of their daily existence, it is surprising how little they know about it. If someone was to take down the white pictures of Jesus in some black churches, the person would most probably be thrown out or chastised severely. Some black churches are getting the message, and placing a black Jesus on their walls using scriptural descriptions of his appearance as justification. Read, *"Egypt and Christianity"* by John G. Jackson. A black child reared in a black church, seeing a white Christ, and being told to "fear" God, receives a subconscious message. When that same child experiences racism, that fear surfaces because the antagonist is also white. Jesus Christ was black as was Virgin Mary. "The word, Christ, comes from the Indian, Krishna or Chrishna, which means 'The Black One'."[7] Europeans changed the images. This fact is well known throughout the world. The Pope visits the Shrine of the Black Madonna in Poland on occasion. At one time, all Madonnas were black. If a black woman was worshiped as the mother of Christ, would it not stand to reason that Christ being the son of Mary was also black? We do not begin to see a white Jesus until 1505 when Pope Julius II commissioned Michelangelo to paint biblical figures Europeans could identify with. How can this be denied? An excellent book on the subject is, *"What Color Was Jesus?"* by William Mosley.

Upon the walls of the Catacombs of Rome, stands three figures, Jesus, Isaiah and a White woman. Both men are pictured black. No one knows when this drawing was done and by whom, but we are sure that whoever drew it so very long ago, knew historically that they could not have been of a Caucasian persuasion (as indicated by Dr. Asa Hilliard in his presentation "Free Your Mind: Return to the Source; African Origins of Civilization"). In fact, Moses was exposed to the Papyrus of Ani (containing the Principles of MAAT), while attending school in Africa which was the educational seat of the world in his time. So did he actually receive the Ten Commandments while on the mountain, or was he enlightened to 10 of the 42 that were applicable to his people at the time? Where does deception end and truth begin in Western distortions? A periodical containing the complete Egyptian hieroglyphics and translation is, *"The Book of the*

Dead, the Papyrus of Ani", by E.A. Wallis Budge, curator of the British Museum. Another book every home should have is *"Moses and Monotheism"*, by Sigmund Freud.

Young minds absorb like sponges. They can see and understand a lot of what is in the world. But they may not understand why lies were necessary to keep their people down. They surely know white people control the world, possess the best of everything, dictate law and enforce it (white policemen), and heaven knows they have never seen a black president. So Blacks need to reconsider the strategies and teach their children the truth. Black youth need to know how to survive at a time and in a place that has little regard for them or their longevity. They need to know the struggle for truth and justice is still being fought by their parent's generation. They also need guidance for future struggles. They need to know their most reverent heroes were black like them, even in the field of medicine.

The beginnings of the practice of medicine began with black people also. Black youth and adults need to know about Imhotep, the first physician known to man. He was physician to King Zoser (2980 B.C.-Golden Age-6th Dynasty). The Greeks renamed him Aescalapius. He was the true father of medicine. The book to read is, *"Imhotep: The Vizier and Physician of King Zoser and Afterwards the Egyptian God of Medicine"* by Jamieson Hurry. How would it make black youth feel to know someone like them was the first to practice medicine. But, medicine was but one great innovation.

How about law? MAAT was the law. Moral and legal wrongs were one and the same, not like today with division between church and state. In fact, today's laws were instituted on ancient principles, but the Western majority has been negligent in revealing this truth to the masses. The proof resides within Egyptian pyramids. Upon pyramid walls, are images left for future generations. Images of black Africans and their accomplishments. Images of their tremendous wealth, glory, beauty, mathematical genius, superb writings and beliefs. The oldest book in the world is etched there. Read, *"The lost Pharaohs of Nubia"* by Bruce Williams. There are also bodies of black mummies within their tombs (They have been taken to the Cairo Museum). This has also been proven by Dr. Cheikh Anta Diop from

Senegal. Mummies with closely packed melanin in their derm (skin) proved they were black. This crucial knowledge was brought to light by Dr. Asa Hilliard, a professor at Georgia State University. He has lectured extensively on our Egyptian ancestry. His lecture, (Free Your Mind) is extremely enlightening. He speaks of Tutankhamen, an Egyptian Pharaoh, commonly known as King Tut. He was a black pharaoh of little significance, but black nonetheless. His parents were also black. Read about him in *"Tutankhamen"* by Edward L. Jones. Also *"Black Egypt and Her Negro Pharaohs"* by Sterling M. Means. Black queens also ruled Egypt. For further information, read *"The Great Queens of Ethiopia"* by Larry Williams and Charles S. Finch, and *"Black Women in Antiquity"* by Ivan Van Sertima.

Another black Pharaoh of note, is Akhenaten. His marriage to a foreigner changed the total belief system of Egypt. His bride, Nefertiti (possibly from a northern semitic culture) believed in one God. During this time period, Egyptians had many gods. They believed in anthropomorphic gods (gods in human form walking among them-Pharaohs) and prayed to as many gods as there were situations and natural occurrences. There were gods who ruled the sun, moon, planting, harvesting, love, war, etc. Read, *"The Gods of the Egyptians"* or, *"Studies in Egyptian Mythology"* by E.A. Wallis Budge. Nefertiti's influence on Akhenaten, caused a great uproar among his people. He designated the one and only true God, the one introduced to him by his wife, as the only god to be worshipped in Egypt.[8]

What about art? We're told of great Grecian and Roman art in western schools, but no one reveals their origins. The Pantheon in Athens is considered one of the great wonders of the world, yet, it is a copy of an African religious site, Carnak Temple, almost three times its size. All Grecian and Roman statues, gods, goddesses, myths and fables were of African origin. Aesop was an African spinner of folklore. For detailed information read, *"Black Zeus: African Mythology and History"*, by Edward L. Jones, *"Art in Ancient Egypt"*, by C. Alfred, *"Art from the Age of Akhenaten"* by R.A. Fazzini, and *"A Book of the Beginnings*: *Containing an Attempt to Recover and Reconstitute the Lost Origins of the Myths and Mysteries, Types and Symbols, Religion and Language, with Egypt for the Mouthpiece and Africa as the Birthplace"* by Gerald Massey.

Black people need to become aware of black rulers and empires that existed in Bilad-as-Sudan (land of the Blacks-the Sudan). Read, *"History of African Civilization"* by E. Jefferson Murphy to encounter the glorious regal splendor of Ghana, Mali and Songhai.

Murphy describes the richness of Ghana by quoting eighth-century Arab astronomer al-Fazari who called it "The land of gold." He also quoted Arab geographer, al-Ya'qubi as saying; "There is the kingdom of Ghana. Its king is mighty, and in his land are gold mines. Under his authority are various other kingdoms and in all of this region there is gold." Murphy uses an account from al-Bakri's "Kitab al Masalik wa'l Mamalik" (written in 1062) for further insight on Ghana's king:

The king adorns himself like a woman, wearing necklaces and bracelets, and when he sits before the people he puts on a high cap decorated with gold and wrapped in turbans of fine cotton. The court of appeal is held in a domed pavilion around which stand ten horses with gold embroidered trappings. Behind the king stand ten pages holding shields and swords decorated with gold, and on his right are the sons of the subordinate kings, all wearing splendid garments and with their hair mixed with gold. On the ground around him are seated his ministers, whilst the governor of the city sits before him. On guard at the door are the dogs of fine pedigree, wearing collars of gold and silver adorned with knobs...the royal audience is announced by the beating of a drum which they call "deba" made out of a long piece of hollowed-out wood. When the people have gathered, his co-religionists grow near upon their knees, sprinkling dust upon their heads as a sign of respect, whilst the Muslims clap hands as their form of greeting. The king who governs them at present is called Tenkaminen; he came to the throne in A.H. 455. Tenkaminen is the master of a large empire and a formidable power. The king of Ghana can put 200,000 warriors in the field, more than 40,000 being armed with bow and arrow.[9]

Murphy used personal accounts by world traveler, Ibn Battuta (fourteenth century) to describe Mali:

My stay at (the capital of Mali) lasted about fifty days; and I was shown honor and entertained by its inhabitants. It is an excessively hot place, and boasts a few small date palms, in the shade of which they sow watermelons. Its water comes from underground waterbeds at that point and there is plenty of mutton to be had. The garments of its inhabitants are of fine Egyptian fabrics. Their women are of surpassing beauty, and are shown more respect than the men. The state of affairs among these people is indeed extraordinary. Their men show no signs of jealousy whatever. No one claims descent from his father, but on the contrary from his mother's brother. A person's heirs are his sister's sons, not his own sons. This is a thing which I have seen nowhere in the world except among the Indians of Malabar. But those are heathens; these people are Muslims, punctilious in observing the hours of prayer, studying books of law, and memorizing the Koran. Their women show no bashfulness before men and do not veil themselves, though they are assiduous in attending the prayers. Any man who wishes to marry one of them may do so, but they do not travel with their husbands, and even if one desired to do so her family would not allow her to go.

The Negroes possess some admirable qualities. They are seldom unjust, and have a greater abhorrence of injustice than any other people. Their sultan shows no mercy to anyone who is guilty of the least act of it. There is complete security in their country. Neither traveler nor inhabitant in it has anything to fear from robbers. They do not confiscate property of any white man who dies in their country, even if it be uncounted wealth. On the contrary, they give it into the charge of some trustworthy person among the whites, until the rightful heir takes possession of it. They are careful to observe the hours of prayer, and assiduous in attending them in congregations, and in bringing up their children to them. On Fridays, if a man does not go early to the mosque, he cannot find a corner to pray in, on account of the crowd.[10]

Murphy described King Mansa Kankan Musa's (of Mali) pilgrimage to Mecca in 1324:

This expedition excited the attention of the entire Islamic world because of its size, pageantry and enormous wealth. Musa's arrival in Cairo was preceded by five hundred slaves, each carrying a six-pound staff of gold. Next came Musa and his retainers, followed by a caravan of one hundred camels, each carrying three hundred pounds of gold. Hundreds of other camels carried food, clothing, and other supplies. Visitors were required to prostrate themselves before the sultan, and Musa claimed this would be impossible for an emperor of his rank and power. He finally agreed to a face-saving compromise in which he prostrated himself before the sultan as the agent of Allah, not as a mundane ruler. The wisely appreciative sultan immediately recognized Mansa Musa as an equal and had him sit beside him for a long discussion.[11]

According to Murphy, Cairo administrative official al-Omari gave this account of Mansa Musa's visit twelve years later:

This man (Mansa Musa) spread upon Cairo the flood of his generosity: there was no person, officer of the court, or holder of any office of the Sultanate who did not receive a sum of gold from him. The people of Cairo earned incalculable sums from him, whether by buying and selling or by gifts. So much gold was current in Cairo that it ruined the value of money. Let me add that gold in Egypt had enjoyed a high rate of exchange up to the moment of their arrival. The gold mitqal that year had not fallen below twenty-five drachmas. But from that day onward, its value dwindled; the exchange was ruined, and even now it has not recovered. The mitqal scarcely touches twenty-two drachmas. That is how it has been for twelve years from that time, because of the great amounts of gold they brought to Egypt and spent there.[12]

Songhai ruler, Sunni Ali, is often captioned as the important ruler of the Songhai kingdom. His military conquests "converted Songhai into a true empire", says Murphy. But Askia Toure' took Songhai to its final glory. Murphy described his feats:

Askia Muhammed built the Songhai Empire into the largest and most powerful force in the western and central Sudan. His armies pushed the borders of the declining Mali Empire back to the Malinke heartland. It is believed that Songhai troops seized Niani, Mali's capital, at least briefly.

In the east, they conquered several Hausa states, and fought a few inconclusive battles with the only Sudanic force that could match their strength, the army of the great Kanem-Bornu Empire, based far away in the Lake Chad region. Control of the lands along the Niger, from Malinke to Hausa country, freedom from raids by Tuareg and Mossi, and the rule of Songhai governors stationed far into the Sahara, made the Songhai Empire a vast commercial power as well as a political and military force.[13]

Toure' also made a hajj (pilgrimage) to Mecca. He carried 3,000 pieces of gold, was accompanied by 500 horsemen and 1,000 foot soldiers. Read, *"Journey of the Songhai People"* by Napendo Ulinzi Milele.

Black youth of today demonstrate superior creativity in their African approach to self adornment, music, rhythmic rap, and in just about every area of their lives. As can be seen above, they are descendants of a great people. Their innate capabilities to create have been copied by every medium. This, as has been clearly shown, is no accident. The beauty and power they possess is envied by majority youth. There is no response in kind, so imitation occurs. This should indicate to black youth how crucial they are in setting the pace for future developments not only in entertainment, but also in the sciences and business.

It would have seemed impossible for our ancestors to build pyramids, create empires, start the practice of medicine and law, but they did. They took impossible dreams and breathed life into them. Today, it may seem impossible for black people to eradicate responses to racism and racism itself, but it can be done. The first step is to know self. Study the true history of the first people to grace the earth. Inhale all the glory gleaned from filling the mind and soul with the food of past cultural and societal accomplishment, stolen from us by those who used us for economic gains. Read, *"Stolen Legacy"* by George James. Once satiated with knowledge of self, inspiration comes, self-esteem forces the chest outward and the head high, brothers and sisters become vital vessels to be filled with information lost and now found, babies become future couriers and successors, hopelessness ends, helplessness becomes a helping hand, communities become havens of support, drugs become unnecessary, crime obsolete, and families crucial.

II

THE BLACK FAMILY

The black family can be broken down into five categories: nuclear, extended, communal, national and universal.

Nuclear families are comprised of immediate family members, such as; father, mother, children, or single parents and unconventional family structures that are becoming the norm in America today. Families considered unconventional are gay households with children, adoptive single parents and stepparent households. Read, *"Black Families in White America"* by Andrew Billingsley and, *"Informal Adoption Among Black Families"* by Robert B. Hill.

The structure is not as important as the substance within each. The values exhibited with each household are key. Are the parents proud of who they are? Are they instilling self-pride, decency, knowledge of self, respect for others and unconditional love? Read, *"The Strengths of Black Families"* by Robert B. Hill. If these values are taught at home, a child will carry them wherever they go. If they wander into a situation debasing their culture, heritage and / or race, they will respond in the proper way. Their first reaction would be to correct false impressions by relating the truth of who they are. If further harassment takes place, they will walk away with dignity. That is the ideal scenario any parent would glorify in, but in order for it to become a reality, children must be given guidance. All parents

reading this need just think back in time when such an incident oc-
curred in their lives. How did you react? Did you want to fight ("those
are fighting words"), were your feelings hurt and you in turn wanted
to hurt the abuser? Of course they were, and most probably you did
retaliate.

Children today are no different. What will make them different
will be the psychological tactics we teach them instead of physical
ones. Both parents must be on one accord. They must communicate
how they want their children to be reared, support each other when
making decisions, and fervently standing by those decisions. One
parent permitting violent behavior and the other advocating non-vio-
lence, confuses children. This issue should be addressed before marriage, not in the throes of a tempestuous situation. Children, by nature, will try to meet parent's expectations. This is their way of pleas-
ing their parents. If they do not know what is expected of them, don't
expect a desired behavior. Case in point:

A young mother dressed her four-year-old, and took him to a friend's
home. She didn't tell the child where he was going, nor did she prepare
him for what was to take place. (The child was not told what was expected
of him).

Upon arrival at her friend's house, he became very unruly. He whined,
stood upon the couch and jumped onto the cocktail table, breaking the
glass insert. The young mother couldn't understand it. Her son had not
displayed this type of behavior at home. She hurriedly apologized, made
arrangements to replace the broken glass, and scurried her little menace
home.

Had the young woman told the child where they were going,
and how she expected him to behave, more effort would have been
made on the child's part to please his mother. If the child has behavioral problems, this approach may not work. But the main point here
is, preparation. Eradicating the unknown, which causes fear, and instilling the known, or, expected. This approach works in children of
all ages. Of course adolescence is a difficult behavioral period, but
with chiding and light horseplay, they too can deliver for they also
aim to please their parents.

Racism attacks on many sides. Television is a major battle front for parents to take control of. Read, *"Blacks and White TV: Afro-Americans in Television Since 1948"* by J. Fred MacDonald.

Cartoons are violent and have racial undertones. Dark sinister characters are upended by blond-haired, blue-eyed saviors. This must be explained to children to make them aware of subliminal messages coming through. Very young children should only be permitted to watch shows previewed by parents in advance due to their limited level of understanding.

Sitcoms often-times over exaggerate family life. These should also be monitored by parents. All white families do not live trouble-free existences with minor problems and happy-go-lucky personalities as these shows profess. Parents must be ever watchful that life's realities are not being distorted by this medium, and when they are, point it out to the child/children.

They must be taught that commercial ads on television are simply businesses competing to relieve them of monies better saved or spent on necessities. When these same businesses advertise needed products without black representation, the products should not be purchased. The writing of letters by black viewers to these companies indicating why their products are not being purchased, may open doors for black actors.

News and news magazine shows are the most psychologically damaging television fair, because of their sensationalism of events, especially those highlighting black crime.

Parents should watch the news with their children on a daily basis. Many misinterpretations of the truth are related to the masses through this format. Negative images of black people run rampant be it crime, welfare, or Aids. Not long ago, reporters reported more black people had Aids than any other group in America. This is virtually impossible. Of the 290 million people in America, 28-40 million are black. There are eight times more white gay men than black. If reporters had reported more black people had Aids by "ratio" than whites, the statistic might be believable. In their rush to demean Blacks one more time, they shot themselves in the foot. Astute minds within the populace know better, it's the ones that do not that can cause problems. Comparing by "ratio" simply means, comparing two things in proportion to each other. The number of black Aids victims within the black population as opposed to the number of white Aids victims in the white population. There are more white Aids victims overall, but there are not as many in the larger white population as there are black Aids victims within the smaller black population. Even using the "Ratio" statistic leaves room for doubt. So what is the underlying message here? "White folks, don't cohabitate with Blacks, they more than likely have Aids."

Newscasters play many games with our children's minds. Another game is crime.

Black men alleged to have committed a crime have been described as, "possible drug dealer", "thug", "beast", "huge black", "street hoodlum", "animal", and many names too humiliating to state here, and are penalized to the full extent of the law. A white man in Boston, after having killed his pregnant wife, stated a black man committed the crime. When the black community protested the harsh treatment leveled upon it during the police search for the illusional man, further investigation proved otherwise. Seeing no way out, the man committed suicide rather than face the consequences he intended for someone black. How overwhelming are the statistics on these types of events? How many black men are incarcerated due to white men who use majority attitudes and stereotypes to their advantage? Black men bear the brunt of society's anguish. These men are the unfortunate of the unfortunate, yet, they are debased. White men committing heinous crimes such as: mass murder, sexual abuses on multiple children, murder and dismemberment of bodies, and others we are all aware of, are called unfortunate souls from dysfunctional backgrounds. If they are indeed entitled to mercy, and/ or insanity defenses, then men of color reared in a racist, dysfunctional society without real equal opportunity should be measured by the same yardstick.

Books kids are exposed to as toddlers can also do them damage. Fairy tales such as Mother Goose Tales, Grimm's Fairy Tales, and typical stories with white heroes and characters, program black children's minds to a white world absent of black heroes that they can identify with. African story books are available, please purchase them instead. Black children should be identifying with what is real for them. Aesop's Fables are excellent. Each story has a moral to it. Aesop lived over twenty-five centuries ago. Greek writers, Herodotus, Plutarch, Planudes and Jean de La Fantaine described him as flat-nosed, thick-lipped and black-skinned. His name was also changed from the African (unknown) to Esop, which means "Ethiopian". He was a slave owned by Xantus and Idamon (Greeks). Idamon let him earn his freedom by hiring him out to entertain. He was loved by Croesus (King of Lydia) and spun his tales at his court. He was thrown off a cliff by Delphi citizens because of his influence over Croesus regarding their monetary needs. He left a treasure in tales to be enjoyed worldwide. Many black children having heard his stories, are unaware of his race and life. Read, *"The Negro in History"* by U.S. Army Adjutant General School.

Black children are being exposed to majority influences within the environment. Do we think they cannot see the dichotomy between black and white? These distortions need to be explained so they can be fully armored with truth and the reality of who they are dealing with, and will have to deal with for the rest of their lives if they choose to stay in this country.

Movies are closing in at an astronomical pace. More movies than ever before are bombarding society. They have to be monitored v-e-r-y closely. Read, *"From Sambo to Superspade: The Black Experience in Motion Pictures"* by Daniel J. Leab and, *"Toms, Coons, Mulattoes, Mammies, and Bucks: An Interpretive History of Blacks in American Film"* by Donald Bogle and, *"Slow Fade to Black: The Negro in American Film 1900-1942"* by Thomas Cripps. (The study in Dr. Thomas Cripps book introduces the reader to early black films seldom seen. This author's study under Dr. Cripps at Morgan State University proved fascinating and highly enlightening). Many movies of the past do not have any black people in them. If a black person is in a movie without a starring role, we immediately know they will be killed off. This is Hollywood's mentality. Racism shines through with the merciless destruction of the "disposable ones". Since it is a reflection of a larger society, Hollywood doesn't see itself as committing a disservice to a large segment of its patrons. It is just normal filmmaking procedure. Parents and children need to be encouraged to write letters demanding their image be shown in a positive light. They should also be encouraged to pursue careers in film as entrepreneurs. When these things have been brought to their attention, who knows how many Spike Lees will materialize. They also must be taught to bide their time when immediate upward mobility seems impossible. When stagnation occurs, time should be spent honing their skills to maximum potential. When an opportunity arises; one must be ready to plunge.

Black families should also create foundations to support responsible family members with loans to start businesses. Entrepreneurship is the battle cry of the 90's. No longer can blacks depend on majority banks to support their dreams. Statistics show they lay out impossible criteria for black people to meet to secure loans, and at higher interest rates. The government has finally begun to intervene in this area. One nuclear family can coordinate with the extended family to start such a foundation. Each family would pool money into the foundation (tax exempt at this time). The proceeds from this collective fund will be used for education of children and business loans at a low rate of interest. This would afford all family members an education and a chance to become entrepreneurs.

The extended family must support all its members. Extended families are comprised of grandparents, great-grandparents, aunts, uncles, cousins, in-laws (all), nieces, nephews, etc. When one member of a family has a dream, support them. Encourage him or her to become the best that they can without envy or competitiveness. A little competition is good, as long as it's positive. Family reunions should be planned to transact important family business such as: starting up a foundation (mentioned earlier) and tracking genealogical information about the family. This history is extremely important. All black families need to know as much as they can about their family history. Precious documents can be lost due to paper corrosion. If ever a time comes that reparations are to be paid to former slave families, could you prove your family was enslaved in America? Be ready for this ever growing possibility.

Family networking for schools, jobs and professional contacts is crucial. No one will ever know all the people their relatives know. And don't underestimate who a relative might know. Many paths cross in life. Case in point:

A young lady wanted to work in City Hall as a clerk. It seemed a highly prestigious job to her. After two years of placing applications every six months rendered no response, she reluctantly ceased in her efforts to pursue the job she dreamed of having.

Her stepfather often dropped her off at work in the mornings, before heading to the plant where he worked. One morning while taking her to work, he asked if she had gotten a promotion in the factory yet. She said no. She went on to say she didn't want to work there any more and would rather work in City Hall where some of her High School classmates were employed, but after applying four times, she was never called in for an interview.

His mouth fell open, then he threw his head back and laughed. He told her he and the mayor were old classmates and met over coffee every morning before work, and getting her an interview was no problem. She was interviewed a week later, and a job was created for her. Let people know what your hopes and dreams are.

Communal families are families within a given community, and each family is concerned about everyone within the community. If a child errs in some way and its parents are not available, an adult within the community takes charge and verbally corrects the child in a respectful way. Crime cannot take place in such a place. Everyone looks out for everyone else. This does not mean getting involved in another family's business. It simply means being watchful of strangers, protecting children, and being sources of inspiration and encouragement for everyone like family. This type of family is important because sometimes children feel freer asking questions of someone other than their parents. Of course parents would want their children to come to them when perplexed about something, but sometimes they may want different points of view. Communal families are also important because they share the same environmental space. Communties stand together for better schools, ecological concerns, crime reduction and the safety of their children and homes. Black communities need to come together. Meetings should be held to determine where a community stands and how it can be improved. Efforts should then be made to improve it. If it means community patrols, picketing, or town meetings, it should be done. This demonstrates to children that people can make things better for themselves without depending on outside forces.

The national family is the total of black families in America experiencing this diaspora together. Personal experiences are as diversified as the hues of brown, yet, they have racism as their common enemy whether all of them realize it or not. The main objective of the national family is to advance in spite of the obstacles confronting it. Read, *"Cultural Bases of Racism and group oppression: An Examination of Traditional "Western" Concepts, Values and Institutional Structures Which Support Racism, Sexism and Elitism"* by J. L. Hodge D. K. Struckmann, and L.D. Trost. All blacks may not agree on most things, but they can most assuredly agree that self determination is the wave of the future. This being so, there must be a collective effort to employ the underemployed and unemployed.

This is not in the framework of the usual way of doing business, but rather unorthodox. For instance, a black employer employs two High School drop outs. They are taught how to become reliable employees, encouraged to attend night school, and further their education in college for a higher position in the business with a raise (incentive). Two lives would be saved from a mediocre condition and may possibly make outstanding contributions. Blacks have to sacrifice to help one another. An example of what can be accomplished can be seen in Los Angeles where rival gangs have made a complete turnaround and are now working together to better their communities. And this is because someone like Jim Brown showed them someone cared about them and their future. Problems will arise, and that's to be expected when an unstructured, disorganized person is challenged to change his or her habits. With patience, and eyes on the prize, black employers will win many souls for the struggle. Even those who falter will not be lost, for the seed would have been planted, and they will know someone cares.

The homeless brothers and sisters refusing to come in from the cold, need blankets and food on a regular basis. They will not go away, neither will some of them ever again become players in this society. These poor souls also need care. If but a few brothers and sisters take the time to say a kind word, give a few pennies, or provide a decent meal once in a while, it would be tonic for the soul. No one should be denied love.

Prisons have claimed a large segment of our brotherhood. They too are a part of this diaspora. They need more than religion during their confinement. They need programs designed by Blacks while they are behind prison walls. They need training after release, and they need jobs. We must not be afraid to help them. In most cases environmental factors (that a large number of black people escaped in the 60's and 70's) breeded them. We cannot have lives devoid of crime if the cancer that causes it has not been cured. Blacks must root it out of their communities by providing alternatives, and rehabilitate those who feel they have no other recourse. They must, however, weed out the hard core element that resist change.

Individuals speaking for the people in the national arena, must be selected by the people. Glory hungry opportunists must be ignored. The government, nor the press should be allowed to decide who leads black people. Voices should cry out in alarm in the form of letters and boycotts when this occurs. Black people should be too wise at this juncture to be duped by imposters utilizing the people's causes for monetary gains, Board of Director positions, influence, and/or power. If a voice chosen to speak for black people is silenced, another from their ranks will step forward, and another, and another, until the message is clear that a body may die, but the struggle lives on through all black people. A national agenda is necessary, for collectively we rise and disunity breeds failure.

The universal family is in trouble. Many brothers and sisters around the world are in dire turmoil. Their countries are in distress due to famine, Aids, coup d'etats and racism. The colonial imperialists left a legacy of strife and confusion. Greater efforts must be put forth to bridge the gap internationally. The Pan-African movement has made strides, but needs assistance. Every black community on the planet has suffered some form of European oppression. The manifestations of past oppressive horrors are merely coming into fruition. Read, *"How Europe Underdeveloped Africa"* by Walter Rodney.

We are not sure where Aids first developed, or how. But we do know that it is eating up the African population at an astounding rate. There are theories surrounding its development in European labs in strategic areas, for the most part, Africa. The theory that it was scientifically designed to kill black people (they die much quicker than do whites), has not yet been proven. Read, *"Journey Of the Songhai People"* by Napendo Ulinze Milele. We have cause for paranoia, for the past does not put Caucasians in good stead. Just as the Jews have not forgotten The Holocaust, we have not forgotten slavery and the Tuskegee syphilis experiments. It would do us an injustice if they think we have forgotten the slaughter of Malcolm X (and the government tie-in), assassination of Martin Luther King, inexplicable demise of Whitney Young, swift expiration of Harold Washington, assassination of the Kennedys, imprisonment of Nelson Mandela, massacre of the children of Soweto, destruction of Steven Biko, revenge on Huey Newton (if you don't believe their story of how he died), and so many more.

The universal collective consciousness of the black family must assuage itself in spirituality to maintain sanity and forgive such terrible inhumane treatment. It must direct itself into positive arenas of hard work in the above areas to wring out the rage seething within. It has to will up its hate unto the heavens, for God's revenge is sweeter. It must continue to survive and strive, for the story is to be continued...

III

FORMAL EDUCATION

Educational institutions in America have consistently ignored black contributions made during the development of this country, and continue to eliminate textbooks containing this information. Until inclusion, the responsibility lies with the black community to disseminate this information to black children encouraging them to reach their maximum potential.

During the 1950's, two great black men were included in textbooks; Booker T. Washington and George Washington Carver. Their inclusion was inevitable due to the high exposure they enjoyed nationally. Not too many years ago, Crispus Attucks was included as also being of African descent.

The intentional exclusion of Blacks was part of a design to culturally assimilate black people into the "Melting Pot" of America to assume European cultural mores, and to instill white superiority. This plan did not work.

Black Americans are demanding truth. Why is it a necessity for children (black and white) to know about these individuals? The answer is vital to all Americans. There has been and continues to be a few role models like those mentioned above for black and white children to relate to. White children need exposure to black role models in order to develop respect for people unlike themselves. Most white children's world is exclusively "white". In a multiracial society, people must be exposed to each other if understanding and harmony is to be achieved. Read, *"The 'Rightness of Whiteness': The World of the White Child in a Segregated Society"* by Abraham F. Citron, and *"The Miseducation of the Negro"* by Carter G. Woodson". Some people would argue the above due to integration having been implemented. But closer scrutiny will reveal the tribal makeup of most communities and schools in America.

White children are led to believe their forefathers discovered, created, and invented everything useful in society. This myth has not been corrected. Below are some of the black inventors and their inventions. Without their contributions, the industrial revolution would not have been successful.

Some Black inventors and their inventions:

M.W. Binga-Street sprinkling apparatus, 1879, **A.B. Blackburn**-Railway signal, 1888, **H. Blair**-Corn planter, cotton planter, 1834 & 1836, **J.E. Matzelier**-(Mechanism for distributing tacks, 1899- Mailing machine, 1896-Tack separating mechanism, 1890-Lasting machine, 1891), **E. McCoy**

> Lubricator for steam engines-1872
> Steam lubricator-1874
> Ironing Table-1874
> Steam cylinder lubricator-1876
> Lawn sprinkler design-1899
> Steam dome-1885
> Lubricator attachment-1887
> Lubricator for safety valves-1887
> Drip cup-1891

W.B. Purvis

> Bag fastener-1882
> Hand stamp-1883

Fountain Pen-1890
Electric railway-1894
Magnetic car balancing device-1895
Electric railway switch-1897
10 paper bag machines-1884-1894

G.T. Woods

Steam boiler furnace-1884
Telephone transmitter-1884
Apparatus for Transmissions of Message by Electricity-1885
Relay instrument-1887
Polarized relay-1887
Electro mechanical brake apparatus-1887
Electro magnetic brake apparatus-1887
Railway telegraphy-1887
Induction telegraph system-1887
Tunnel construction for electric railway-1888
Galvanic battery-1888
Automatic safety cut-out for electric circuits-1889
Electric railway system-1891
Electric railway supply system-1893
Electric railway conduit-1893
System of electrical distribution-1896
Amusement apparatus-1899

Garrett A. Morgan

Gas mask-1914
Automatic traffic light-1923

Blacks in other fields have also been ignored. For further information read, *"Blacks in Science: Astrophysicist to Zoologist"* by Hatti Carwell, *"Negroes in Science: Natural Science Doctorates, 1876-*

1969" by James M. Ray, *"Black Mathematicians and Their Works"* by V.K. Newell, J.H. Gipson, Waldo Rich and B. Stubblefield, *"Black American Scholars: A Study of Their Beginnings"* by Horsemann Fon and *"Black Women in White America: A Documented History"* Edited by Gerda Lerner.

If the average black child was aware of the multiple men and women making contributions that looked like them, imagine the impact it would have on their desire to carry on the great tradition of succeeding in spite of the odds. The information given here can be used by them to educate teachers and classmates.

Since school systems throughout America have been negligent in bringing information to students, the burden falls upon parents, extended families, communal and national families. Black children need "culturing". Education about their people's sojourn in America is vital. As indicated in a prior chapter, self identity is of primary concern. Once that has been achieved, education becomes primary.

Elementary school is the first place their minds are distorted. They are taught American History, writing, reading, introduction to various books, arithmetic, science, art, music and geography. This curriculum is based on a European white middle class ideology. Close monitoring of curriculums will enable parents in educating their children correctly. A culturally educated parent's input is crucial, for the child is subconsciously waiting to hear what part someone like themselves played in the scheme of past national events in a classroom situation. If this information is not forthcoming, disinterest sets in. Constantly being reminded of what other people have done, leaves a black child bored and embarrassed in front of white classmates relishing in their superior glory. Black parents must fill the void.

Parents must scan the textbooks to reacquaint themselves with the information. While assisting their children with homework, they can interject information about black contributions. If this technique is not successful, study groups can be held in various homes in the community. Snacks should be provided to add to a light fun-filled atmosphere. Remember, learning can be fun! Games such as "Identity" can be played (sold in ethnic and department stores), or games can be created by parents. The main purpose is to inform.

The monitoring process should take place throughout a child's educational years, especially during High School when interest wanes considerably. Asking older children to run study groups for elementary school aged children is a good way to reinforce information.

Black colleges have produced a large number of influential high achievers. College-aged students should be encouraged to apply. These schools provide excellent curriculums with the added ingredient of racial pride, cultural diversity and genuine concern for each students' success. White colleges and universities are not equipped to give black young adults the necessary tools to survive in a racist society. By the time black students reach college age, they have immense knowledge of white culture and what is expected of them by majority standards. They now need support and encouragement that only a black college, or university can provide. This does not mean graduate study at Yale or Harvard should not be a goal. This is subjective. If a student feels ready to deal with the attitudes of individuals wishing them ill, and can bear the burden, their efforts are to be commended. They too need support from family, friends and communities. The main objective is to lessen stress factors, thus permitting energies once spent proving worthiness to be channeled toward more positive pursuits. Black students at some white colleges and universities are constantly maligned with "Nigger Nights", physically abused and made to feel unwanted. These distractions affect concentration on studies, a sense of well being, and leaves feelings of helplessness and inadequacy.

Textbooks at this level are directed to "white" patterns of thinking and experiences. Cultural identity to subject matter leaves black students far afield.

The struggle continues by the majority to disband black colleges and universities in the guise of them not being needed. They will be needed as long as racism exists in America. Nowhere else can people of color glorify in who they are without retribution or vilification. Upon these campuses, students are culturally understood and accepted for who they are without qualification. The support given black institutions by black people nationally has blessed us with legislators, civil rights leaders, doctors, lawyers, scientists, mayors, a governor, business men and women, and numerous achievers in all segments of society. We must strive to keep these institutions alive and well.

Another area of concentration is the ability of teachers to instruct our children properly. Who would believe in 1993, a white teacher would ask young black children to act as slaves in an imaginary slave market, and for them to be parcelled out to white students as slaves? The teacher did not realize how deeply she injured the children, because her racist attitudes did not take their pain into account. She did not stop to think of the degrading and humiliating position she placed them into in front of white students. How superior did white children feel knowing their people have never been subjected to such a monstrous thing as slavery? Why did the black children have to be reminded of their degradation in such a heinous way? Why wasn't the teacher dismissed immediately instead of being requested by the School Board to offer an apology?

Black parents have to keep an ever vigil eye on every aspect of their children's contact with the educational system. Visits to classrooms with permission from school Principals should be the norm (even if parents have to stand outside of classrooms and listen to what is going on as this author did for many years). Parents should demand racial sensitivity seminars be held in schools to make teachers aware of their limits when dealing with impressionable minds. They should also be investigated thoroughly by School Boards before being hired to work in any school system (some male teachers have been exposed as pedophiles).

Indirect Self-Fulfilling Prophecy is another area black parents must become aware of when evaluating teachers. The teacher's expectations of students inspire students to achieve. Past studies have found that white teachers gave positive facial expressions, gestures and verbal responses to white males more so than white females, black females and black males. The teachers expected white males to succeed therefore the males studied harder in order to meet their teacher's expectations. The response given white females was sweet and positive, but not on as high a level as white males. The expectations of black females was for them to be silent and to behave. Black

males were not expected to perform in any way and were often ignored. Craving for attention, black males began to misbehave. And
we ask why black children are not interested in attending school?
Some black teachers were shown to exhibit the same indirect self-
fulfilling prophecy of students, as above, during the sixties, which
can be attributed to them being influenced by the same societal conditioning. This has changed tremendously throughout the years for
black teachers, because of the civil rights movement and sincere efforts to inspire black achievement.

When Blacks face the fact that no governmental agency, school
board, bureaucracy, or PTA is going to provide what black children
need to get a decent education, they will move politically to do so
themselves. Here again, community demands must be presented to
the proper authorities to create change. No change, no vote!

The struggle for inclusion of black achievement in school textbooks must continue, however. Community groups represent power,
and powerful voices can demand change. School Boards respond to
large communities of tax payers. The rallying call should be made to
all parents, even those of other ethnic groups in integrated communities. With this support, black children will begin to feel secure knowing someone cares and cares enough to confront the institutions causing them pain on a daily basis. With fear aside, more time and effort
can be put into their studies.

Children need exposure to the world beyond their communities
in order to understand why education is important. A child's response
to directives is almost always, "why?". It is better to show them than
to explain. Black children need exposure in a different way than has
been the norm. Their experience has, in the past, been one of seeing
people unlike themselves in leadership and influential positions. This
needs to be changed. When a black child is introduced to a new experience such as visiting the pediatrician's office, the pediatrician should,
if at all possible, be black. The same holds true for visits to the dentist. This is a learning experience also, because the child sees someone like him or herself performing a function they too can aspire to.
The possibility doesn't seem as remote as it may have seemed in the
past from their point of view. School books may have exclusively

contained pictures of white doctors and dentists. The real life experience alters the mental picture and creates a reality they can relate to.

Trips to planetariums, science fairs, conservationist parks, museums, large libraries, art galleries, black art shows, musicals, plays, operas, symphonies and cultural events stimulates their minds. It would be premature to ask a child what they want to grow up to be if they have not been exposed to the possibilities. If parents cannot afford such events, keep track of television listings for programs consisting of the above events. For parents not too thrilled with their children watching television, videos can be rented featuring the above.

Vacations are another educational tool. Children should be exposed to an environment where black people are in charge. The Caribbean and Africa are ideal for this purpose. Of course, children should be at an age (9-up) where they understand what is experienced, and will remember. This adventure will convince them that black people are also capable of running things more than any verbal communication. Transporting a whole family to exotic places is expensive, and may not be the avenue parents wish to choose. Again, videos on these places are available in video stores, although seeing for oneself is more of a significant emotional event. Some families save for years to bring a dream like this into fruition. A few national historical places of interest are:

Historic Sites and Museums

Black American West Museum and Heritage Center, Denver; (303) 292-2566. See how we have played a major role in shaping the American West through historic artifacts, documents, photographs and memorabilia.

Martin Luther King, Jr. Historic Site, Atlanta; (404) 331-5190. Visit King's childhood home on Auburn Avenue, located in what was one of the most prosperous Black communities in the country in the 1930's and 1940's.

DuSable Museum of African American History, Chicago; (312) 947-0600. Learn about the life of Black fur trader and father of the Windy City, Jean Baptiste Point DuSable. The museum also sponsors tours that visit DuSable's landing point and the home of boxer Joe Louis.

Delta Blues Museum, Clarksdale, Mississippi; (601) 624-4461. In the birthplace of bluesmen Muddy Waters and John Lee Hooker is where you'll find this premier music museum.

Harriet Tubman Home, Auburn, New York; (315) 255-3863. The courageous former slave who led more than 300 others to freedom as the underground railroad's most famous "conductor" settled this once major way station for northbound fugitive slaves as her home after the civil war. The house has been preserved as a shrine to her memory.

Bethune Museum and Archives, Washington, D.C.; (202) 332-1233. Feed your mind a spirit at the former home of the civil-rights activist, founder of the National Council of Negro Women and of Bethune-Cookman College in Daytona, Florida. The archives preserves and documents the accomplishments of Black women.

Harpers Ferry National Historical Park, West Virginia; (304) 535-6029. About an hour's drive from Washington, D.C., the Old Town where John Brown led his much-publicized antislavery raid in 1859 has been preserved.

America's Black Holocaust Museum, Inc., Milwaukee; (414) 372-0690. This museum is where you'll find heartrending photographs of our people who died at the hands of lynch mobs, rare books on race relations, posters depicting racial epithets of the past, and slogans that document efforts made to combat racism.

Black Heritage Tours

Montgomery, Alabama's Black Heritage Trail; (800) 252-2262. Tour stops include Tuskegee Institute and W. C. Handy's home.

Barry's Tours and Cruises, San Francisco; (415) 773-9303.

Timpson Limousine & Charter Bus Service, Miami; (305) 756-8551. On one of the tour's main stops, in Coconut Grove, see one of Florida's earliest Black settlements, built in 1889. For history buffs, Dade County's Black Archives History and Research Foundation houses local artifacts and documents.

King-Tisdell Cottage Foundation, Inc., Savannah; (912) 234-8000. The main stop on this center's tour is the Second African Baptist Church, where George Tecumseh Sherman read the Emancipation Proclamation promising displaced slaves 40 acres and a mule.

Boston's Black Heritage Trail; (617) 742-5415. Visit the African Meeting House, built in 1806. This hub of black Boston was the center of the city's abolitionist movement.

Afro-American Historical and Cultural Museum, Philadelphia; (215) 925-0616. Tours visit the Mother Bethel African Methodist Episcopal Church, founded by Richard Allen in 1794, and Allen's Shrine and museum.

Memphis, Tennessee Heritage Tour; (901) 527-3427. Make a historical pilgrimage to Roots author Alex Haley's home in Henning and the Lorraine Motel, where Dr. Martin Luther King, Jr., was slain.

Black History National Recreation Trail, Washington, D.C.; (202) 485-9666. The tour route features the Frederick Douglass National Historic Site, Howard University and Lincoln Park, where you'll see the Emancipation and Mary McLeod Bethune Statues.

(The above was excerpt from "Cultural Caravans" Essence Magazine, February, 1991. Co-authors: Ruth D. Manuel and Valerie Vaz.)

Museums

California Afro-American Museum, Los Angeles, California.; Terrie Rouse-Director.

National Center of Afro-American Artists, Boston, Mass.; Barry Gaither-Director.

Studio Museum in Harlem, New York City, N. Y.; Kinshasha Conwill-Director.

The National Afro-American Museum and Cultural Center, Wilberforce, Ohio.; Dr. John Fleming-Director.

Afro-American Historical Society Museum, Jersey City, N.J.; Ted Brunson-Director.

Children should be taught to visualize already having what they want to achieve. Dreams inspire people to achieve. Children must be encouraged to aspire to achieve something. Small victories build confidence, self-esteem and determination. So, no matter how small their accomplishment, children need parent's praise and "I knew you could do it" responses. When children have a mental picture of a goal, it becomes a dream they strive toward. To them, it is of major importance, and the last thing they want to hear is a parent telling them they do not support their efforts. Even if failure should result, understanding parents can use the experience to teach children how to set attainable goals. This is a tricky thing, because some seemingly impossible feats have been accomplished by little people. The main objective is to not let them lose faith, even in defeat. Black children can and will move into the future as productive human beings with the love, motivation, support and tools provided them by parents, significant others, and concerned community groups. No child need fall by the wayside because no one cares.

The cultural education parents provide in conjunction with school systems (inadequate as they are), is collective formal education. The challenge lies before them. Black children are dropping out of schools at an alarming rate, violence has devastated many schools, teachers cannot maintain control, and the system has broken down. Black parents can reclaim their children, reeducate them, demand change within school systems, demand respect, struggle for inclusion of black heroes in school texts, and pave the way for future advancement. The choice is theirs.

It is idle, a hollow mockery, for us to pray to God to break the oppressor's power, while we neglect the means of knowledge which will give us the ability to break this power. God will help us when we help ourselves.
Frederick Douglass.

Education is our passport to the future, for tomorrow belongs to the people who prepare for it today.
Malcolm X.

Perhaps we shall be the teachers when it is done. Out of the depths of pain we have thought to be our sole heritage in this world- - O, we know about love! And [sic] that is why I say to you that, though it be a thrilling and marvelous thing to be merely young and gifted in such times, it is doubly so, doubly dynamic--to be young, gifted and black.
Lorraine Hansberry.

IV

UNDERSTANDING MAJORITY MENTALITY

Shielding black people from racism in America is an impossi-bility. This being the case, the racist mind should be analyzed and understood by its victims in order to survive its impact.

All majority (white) people in America are racist, and some are comfortable in their racism. This statement is true although many Whites would challenge the validity of it. In "Two Nations", Andrew Hacker indicates 1990 income levels of Whites as opposed to that of Blacks is astronomically higher. White families earning over $50,000 measure 32.5%, while black families earning the same measure 14.5%. On the other end of the scale, white families earning under $15,000 measure 14.2%, while black families earning the same are 37%. The discrepancy clearly shows how much more economically stable Whites are than Blacks. Whites, however, are not yet willing to share that which they have earned off the backs of black free labor over the past three centuries. There is much comfort in being "white" in America and much economic discomfiture in being black.[1] Major-ity people also have deep-rooted fears regarding black rule.

In "The Psychology of Oppression", Joseph H. Baldwin states why Whites approach life differently than Blacks. Whites see America as a place to be dominated in all respects totally disregarding the rights, needs, survival, or cultures of non-European-like peoples. This he terms as the "humanity vs. nature style of operation." The black, or African approach is "humanity-nature unity", or "oneness with nature' style of operation." They must take care of nature for survival's sake. In other words, they must support life in all its manifestations in order for life or nature to sustain them.

Baldwin further states that definitional systems are also different. Whites, when encountering something new (such as countries colonized in the past), could not share what was offered. They had to possess it in totality. Blacks on the other hand, react through feelings, or emotives which does not dictate the taking or possessing, but the sharing, or partaking of that which is offered. These completely diverse approaches to life and people are but one aspect of black refusal to be assimilated into European (used throughout to indicate those having migrated from Europe) value structures. The history of majority people is well known to Blacks due to conditioning, and they cannot see themselves committing destructive acts committed by Whites on other peoples such as was leveled upon Native American Indians, South Africans, Africans and Africans slaves in America.

The main miscalculation made by majority people was in assessing Blacks rejection to European culture. The one possession enslaved Africans had was their cultural identity which was and is natural for them. The maintenance of that identity became crucial for sanity's sake. Even today, the thrust back to cultural identity by youth shows the need to be true to the "natural", or "normal self". A person giving up cultural identity to take on someone else's, becomes two people. In essence, they develop psychosis.

In order to prove his values and cultural superiority, the European had to demean African culture and values making them seem inferior, according to Baldwin. Failure to identify with European values and culture meant failure to obtain and attain rewards in European societies. Those Blacks joining the status quo (displaying pro-racist behaviors) have been termed, "Uncle Toms", or "sell-outs" by Blacks seeking real change and equality.

Caucasian people cannot help how they feel, act and react to black people. It is an intricate part of their makeup, and has been since birth. Their mental programming of superiority began at birth.

As children, most of them lived in a white world without intimate exposure to Blacks. All of their heroes are white, real or unreal. Superman, Samson, Hercules, Alexander the Great, Plato, Alice in Wonderland, Robin Hood, Presidents of the United States, Legislators, Napoleon Bonapart, Kings and Queens , Little Boy Blue, Mother Hubbard, Pied Piper, Goldilocks, Rapunzel, Three little pigs, Little Miss Muffet, Snow White, White Knight in shinning armor, The Wizard of Oz, Dorothy (Wizard of Oz), Jack of beanstalk fame, Cinderella, Billy the Kid, Jesse James, and Santa Claus and his elves. The world revolves around "whiteness", and they cannot see, or refuse to see the detriment this causes to people who are "different" from them. Read, *"The Rightness of Whiteness"* by Abraham F. Cintron.

There are black story books available to add balance to the heroes black children are exposed to. Some of them are:

> *"Lessons From History"* by Jawanza Kunjufu
> *"Huggie Bean"* by Linda Cousins
> *"Brown Spices"* by ABC Coloring Books
> *"Under the Sunday Tree"* by Louise Greenfield
> *"Clean Your Room"* by Harvey Moon
> *"Ghost Writers"* (series) by Deana Ginns
> *"The True Story of the Three Little Pigs"* by Lane Smith
> *"Short Cuts"* by Donald Cruise.
> *"Brother Man Comics"* and *"Ebony Warriors Comics"*
> *"The Afrocentric Self Discovery and Inventory Workbook"* By
>   Useni Perkins
> *"I Look At Me"* by Mari Evans
> *"The Tiger Who Wore White Gloves"* by Gwendolyn Brooks
> *"The Day They Stole The Letter J"* by Jahari Mahiri

Even religious figures on film and in the Bible plunge black children into glorious whiteness. Jesus and his disciples, Moses, Adam and Eve, David and Goliath, Pharaoh, Joshua, Jonah and the Whale, Daniel, Cleopatra, The Holy Family and many others are all white. The true identity of white religious icons are being exposed as African. White resistance to this information indicates the depth of their belief in their superiority. Beneath the beliefs of those possessing the truth (majority scientists, Egyptologists, educators, historians and others), lies fear. Since there have been few European original contributions to the world in music, art, religion and government, they are once again caught in treacherous lies they now scramble to cover up with unsubstantiated data and excuses.

People of color are programmed by the same mechanisms to see white as "purity" and "always winning in the end". Psychologically, they are receiving the message that white is "superior" and everyone else is unimportant, insignificant and secondary. It is no wonder white people cannot see themselves. They gyrate within a world deceptively created for them to believe in. If their beliefs are destroyed by truth (black heroes believed to be white such as Jesus, Moses, Cleopatra, etc.), cognitive dissonance would take place, and Eurocentricity would begin to disintegrate.

During the study of African art, this author entered a museum in Baltimore, Maryland to view an exhibit in the late 80's. Upon seeing Egypt missing in the northeastern African art collection, museum personnel were questioned about its omission. No one could provide an answer. It was obvious that Egypt was purposely being removed (mentally) from its black African roots and set into an Arabic background of achievement (Arabs did not conquer Egypt until the seventh century, Read, *"History of Western Civilization"* by E. Jefferson Murphy). A white woman hearing the conversation, approached the author. She said she thought it strange that Egyptian art was missing also. A conversation, lasting about two hours, ensued. She mentioned her travels worldwide while doing research for her doctoral thesis in fine arts, and during her travels, no art genre could be found that originated in Europe. All art, she continued, came from somewhere else. When questioned about the great art masters of Europe like Renoir, Monet and others, she said they copied the use of colors and toning from other peoples to create an art form. What an enlightening development that was! Museums can be interesting places for exchange of information. This revelation inspired further study that substantiated her findings.

Europeans have imperialistically ravaged other countries,

stolen legacies and people, changed artwork to resemble themselves, modified music, and unsuccessfully tried to bury the truth. Read, *"Sex and Race" Volumes I, II, and III* by Walter Rodney. The Chinese were progenitors of gun powder which has been modified by the European for destructive purposes. The Africans (as noted in chapter 1) contributed law, art, music and government to the world. Each has been modified to serve the colonist's purposes and claimed as his own. Black music is America's only original music form, and African influence is infused in music worldwide.

The unearthing of indisputable evidence of past deceptions has placed Europeans in an awkward position. How can this be explained to the masses of Whites so diligently programmed? What do these deceptions leave majority people to relish in, and how would their children react to them? Their actions, deeds and tribalism are displayed by how their children relate to the world.

A minute number of white children have seen black people entertained in their homes. Their friends are white in their white neighborhoods. The people within their milieu are exclusively white, be it doctors, teachers, store owners, policemen and police chiefs, city fathers, and entertainment hang-outs. School busing and integration impacted on this environment for many years, but recent trends indicate Whites, economically equipped to do so, are moving in large numbers to lily-white neighborhoods and placing their children into private schools. Why? Conscious and, in some cases unconscious racism is the cause. Even they have not analyzed their actions as much as qualifying them. Their common response is flight from drugs and crime, while statistics show drugs and crime run discreetly rampant in the suburbs where they reside. If racism is not the reason for these moves, why are black families attacked with verbal threats, arson and vandalism when moving into these neighborhoods?

Conservative thinking majority people are adamant about keeping things as they are between the races. Their fear outweighs the guilt they feel for past injustices toward people of color. They fear retribution at the hands of Blacks and are more comfortable ignoring requests for equal treatment and equitable distribution of wealth. They subscribe to maintenance of the white race. Interracial procreation is not their mainstay. Their greatest fear is successful commingling of, and procreation between the races. J.A. Rogers speaks on this in "Sex and Race" Volume III:

> While every group has a perfect right to keep to itself if it so decides and to say with whom it will or will not marry, yet the instant it enters the life of another group, so surely does it forfeit that right, and the other group has a right reciprocally to interfere. It is indisputable that in the beginning the black man wished no association whatever with the white, and that the white has forced his company upon him even to the extent of bringing him to America. If the white man will not leave the Negro alone, but wishes to mix with him, the Negro has the perfect right, that is, if there is to be any justice, to say also under what conditions such mixing shall take place.[2]

Zero population growth among whites (for every one that dies, one is born-thus, the anti-abortion movement) has horrifying implications for them. They cringe to think that by the year 2010, there will be more minorities in this country than whites. A large migration of Russians have been streaming into the country since Glastnost, but Haitians are not allowed in. Another phenomenon is the use of female relatives, and females within the population for surrogate birth mothers. Why are so many Caucasian women barren today? God works in mysterious ways. Evidence of this can be found in Deuteronomy 27:15-18:

> 15 "But it shall come to pass, if thou wilt not hearken unto the voice of the Lord thy God, to observe to do all his commandments and his statutes which I command thee this day; that all these curses shall come upon thee, and overtake thee.
>
> 16 Cursed shalt thou be in the city, and cursed shalt thou be in the field.
>
> 17 Cursed shall be thy basket and thy store.
>
> 18 Cursed shall be the fruit of thy body, and the fruit of thy land, the increase of thy kine, and the flocks of thy sheep.

Robert Froman delves deeper into the majority psyche in his book, "Racism". "An individual white in possession of his self-respect is able, in comparing himself with any given individual black, to respect the Black's talents and accomplishments and find them greater than his own without feeling threatened by such a finding. But it seems almost inevitable that a white who lacks self-respect and who is given the chance to concentrate on his identity as a member of a superior race will do so."[3]

In its "Contract with America", the conservatives promise to thwart black advancement, while media attacks consistently program the minds of Whites and other minorities against Blacks. Recent elections of conservatives have thrust the conservative agenda full speed ahead in its efforts to end black upward mobility by cutting social programs instrumental in moving poor people out of poverty and into the work force.

The ultra-Conservative view is one of keeping what has been obtained out of the hands of minorities no matter what the cost. The cost has been the disrobing of their true objectives. 1. Keep black people from upward mobility. 2. If they get anything out of the system, let them get it on their own. 3. Don't assist them in any way. 4. Make it as difficult for them as possible and maybe they will give up. 5. Block them through legislation if possible-if not, hamper enforcement. 6. Divide and confuse them, then destroy their leaders through past and proven methods. As Dick Gregory stated in his album, "The Light Side, The Dark Side", we can just call them "clear people" because we can see right through them. They are the hard-liners refusing to budge an inch. Their fear stems from belief of economic decline for them if minorities are allowed total equality. They truly believe non-whites are inferior. It has been suggested that flight of businesses from America into Mexico and other countries is the beginning of the transfer of wealth because of demographer's warnings of future minority population expansion. These carpetbaggers are in a panic.

Liberals leave room for advancement, that is, until their comfort is threatened. "You can go to school with my daughter, but you can't marry her." Their conciliatory ideology has its limits. When they seem to drift too far left of the whole, they retreat. We owe them much for without their support, many advances would not have been possible. What they need to understand about Blacks, is the need to be able to advance on equal footing with everyone else. Blacks on the whole do not seek equality to marry Caucasians, but if such a union should occur, it shouldn't be considered a major problem. The liberal's usual response is, "but the children will suffer". The core racist begins to surface, and gut level self-evaluation on where the liberal stands is challenged. When it does, hopefully growth will take place. "I, for one, am growing weary of those well-meaning white liberals who are forever telling me they don't know what color I am. The very fact that they single me out at the cocktail party and gratuitously make me the beneficiary of their blessed assurances gives the lie to their pronouncements. My fight is not for racial sameness, it is for racial equality and against racial prejudice and discrimination. I work for the day when my people will be free of the racist pressures to be white like you..". ("We Refuse To Look At Ourselves Through The Eyes of White America" by John O. Killens).[4]

All three groups above seem to think equal rights must be piece-mealed to Blacks. Even though legislation exists, enforcement has been slow and begrudging. It is inevitable that black people will be the forerunners of massive change and spiritual advancement in this country. They happen to believe in "Equality and Justice for All" as do some Whites.

There are majority people in America truly committed to equality for all people. They know they have a vested interest in the success of this experiment called America. They fight alongside the disadvantaged, employ them, assist them and sacrifice much for themselves as well as others. Guilt does not drive these individuals. The sense of right and wrong, plus repulsion to hypocrisy is their motivation. While growing up in America, they believed this country was what it said it was, and since it is not, they strive to make it so. Although all majority people are racist through orientation, some have modified their mental tapes and struggle to rid themselves of racist thoughts and behaviors. They have tuned in to little innuendos and remarks made by hypocritical cronies and associates. They have seen the differences in treatment of Blacks as opposed to Whites. Some of them even know from whence they came. They know all people had one ancestral mother, "African Eve". They have no problem with this. These are the ones Blacks should embrace for they are spiritually aware and passionately believe in the brotherhood of all humanity, and strive to break down personal and institutional racism.

Institutional racism controls the upward advancement of black people and other minorities in the economic and influential arenas within the marketplace. The mentality discouraging inclusion seeks to maintain power and control. They see those deemed "different" as inferior and incapable of playing high stakes monopoly. Although there are now many Blacks in high positions of power in companies and on Boards of Directors, their positioning is for a purpose. Governmental contracts and subsidies are not readily available to large companies showing "lily white" staffing on all levels, especially on executive levels. The "token" positions do not necessarily mean these Blacks have power. More than not, they are well paid show pieces for governmental scrutiny. Many Blacks finding themselves lucky enough to reach such heights, learn all they can in order to compete in the marketplace. They leave to start businesses on their own, and some have become very successful. Others staying, strive for many years never achieving upward mobility. They continuously pound on the "glass ceiling" hoping for inclusion majority power brokers know will never become a reality. Majority businessmen often keep vital/ secret company data out of the hands of executive level Blacks. Closed meetings are the norm, and last minute release of important company strategies is commonplace. Do they really believe this is not being detected? The purpose is clear and obvious. Black businessmen know they must learn the business inside out, token or not. The more they know, the more they may question procedures, tactics and ethics. Majority executives seeking to destroy their competition, or violate the law to reach their goals, do not want someone outside the "inner circle" knowledgeable, and black executives are "outside". They also do not wants Blacks entering into powerful positions by accident due to death, sickness or departure of a majority person. Read, *"Black Life in Corporate America"* by George Davis and Glegg

Watson, and *"Racism and Sexism in Corporate Life"* by Dr. John P. Fernandez.

> White males make up just 39.2 percent of the population, yet they account for 82.5 percent of the Forbes 400 (folks worth at least $265 million), 77 percent of Congress, 92 percent of state governors, 70 percent of tenured college faculty, almost 90 percent of daily-newspaper editors, 77 percent of TV news directors. They dominate just about everything but NOW and the NAACP; even in the NBA, most of the head coaches and general managers are white males.[5]

The federal government is the forerunner in discriminatory practices against people of color. Its responsibility to safeguard the rights of all its people under the constitution has fallen way short of the mark as indicated in the December 14, 1993 Philadelphia Inquirer newspaper article below.

> The federal government, America's biggest employer and supposedly one of its most color-blind, fired minority workers at more than twice the rate of whites last year, official government records show.
> The disparity between whites and minorities existed at every pay grade and for every occupational group, but was greatest among low-level blue-collar and clerical workers, according to Office of Personnel Management statistics obtained by the Inquirer Washington Bureau.
> Overall, minority men were dismissed at more than three times the rate of white's and minority women at double the rate of white's.
> "I don't know what's causing the disparity, or how to solve it," said the government's top personnel official, James B. King, director of the Office of Personnel Management. "But we're going to do the research to get to the bottom of the numbers. Then, if there is a problem, we're going to fix it."

A child could ascertain what is causing the problem. Racism is still embedded in white psyches. And how long is this research going to take? The numbers are indicators that a disparity exists. Since this is so, fix the problem that is evident. This waste of time only delays upward advancement of minorities and during the process of "studying the problem" many more people are being dismissed.

The article further states:

Minorities constituted slightly more than one-quarter of the federal workforce of 2.2 million in 1992, according to OPM figures. But they accounted for more than half of the nearly 12,000 employees dismissed.

OPM statisticians did not distinguish among different minority groups, but four previous, smaller studies of government workers found that blacks were the most frequently fired by a large margin.

Those studies found that more than twice as many blacks as whites were involved in firings and other major discriminatory actions. Asian Americans generally had lower disciplinary rates than whites. Rates for Hispanics and American Indians were comparable to whites or somewhat higher.

After finding blacks in the Internal Revenue Service fired at more than twice the rate of whites in two separate studies in 1991 and 1993, a task force of the National Treasury Employees Union concluded more neutrally that "the problem is largely due to an interaction of cultural forces."

"When a white manager decides a black worker isn't a team player, or has an 'attitude,' that's very subjective," said Brown University sociologist Hilary Silver, who has studied workplace discrimination. "How can you tell if the worker is unmotivated or the lone black in a white setting where subcultural differences are at work?"

California authorities also discovered sharp racial disparities in discipline of state employees in 1987 and have worked to reduce it, said Walter Vaughn, a senior official of the State Personnel Board.

He attributed much of the gap to "inadequate, inconsistent application of workplace rules; racism; lack of appreciation of diversity in the workplace; inadequate selection processes for rank and file supervisors, and inadequate training." [6]

In office settings most majority people collaborate with Blacks to complete work functions, and may attend company social events with them present. Otherwise, Blacks are invisible to them. Many of them will consider black business associates their friend, yet, no outside social camaraderie is evident. Blacks are not invited to their homes, or to holiday functions, such as barbecues or parties. This is not because they purposely omit them. They simply don't think to invite Blacks. It is not normal for them. Blacks, on the other hand, are more open to inviting majority people to their functions. They do not usually distinguish between white and black friends on the whole. In fact, when they find a likable majority person, they tend to think their black friends will like them. A friend is a friend as far as they are concerned. This is not to say all Blacks have white friends. Some are very leery and do not trust majority people at all, and from past experience, with good reason.

Black employees of majority companies are not usually chosen for person-to-person contacts with majority led businesses. White employers prefer majority employees attend meetings and luncheons. The exceptions are when the black employees are the only capable people available and/or the patronage of the company contacted is predominately minority. The thinking on this is that majority people are more comfortable with someone who looks like them. Employers do not want to run the risk of losing business because of racial attitudes. If in the past, an executive happened to be in the company of a businessman and heard negative racial slurs about Blacks, do you think he could transact much business with the guy if he sent a black representative?

Majority people should know how racist they, their families and friends are. If not, all they need do is tune in to themselves and their loved ones using racial slurs, "those people", "nigger" and categorizing all Blacks. This would be like Blacks thinking all white people are cannibals because of Jeffrey Dahmer's appetite for human flesh, especially dark meat.

This categorizing of all black men in their employ, is normal in majority minds. A white transit police chief admitted on television not long ago that while riding the subway he saw two black men standing not far from him. They looked like stereotypical black males (as seen on TV and in movies), so he became guarded. They slowly began walking toward him. He slipped his hand into his coat to retrieve his gun, when one of them said, "Hi Chief". They were his own transit police officers and he hadn't even recognized them out of uniform. Categorization and stereotyping can kill and has many times in the past. He did not see faces, his mind saw "black" and that meant it was time to "fear".

Blacks are beginning to come together economically to achieve their goals. An excellent example is the aid Spike Lee received to finish the film "Malcolm X" from Bill Cosby, Oprah Winfrey and Magic Johnson. More of this kind of cohesion need take place. If the wealthiest among Blacks were to pool 1/3rd of their resources, they could purchase a major motion picture studio in Hollywood to finance important black films. Films are but a tip of the iceberg. Floundering black businesses (once Competitors) could merge thus creating a more solid economic base. Read, *"Black Folks Guide to Making Big Money in America"* and *"Black Folks' Guide to Business* Success*"* by George Subira.

Many majority women are guilty of stereotyping more consistently than any other group in society. They need only see a black man, and fear grips them. They have been programmed to think black men lust after them and will beastly rape and sodomize them. Television news and magazine tabloid shows depict black males as thieves, brutes and animals looking for defenseless white women to ravage. They definitely steer clear of the "yo" type of black boy, or man. Even black men in business suits terrify them. White women strangle their pocketbooks when they see any black man approaching. In their minds, no black man is safe. Why? Innately majority women know most Whites enjoy life's comforts (especially themselves) because of hundreds of years of abuse and misuse of black men and women. They perceive black women to be as weak as themselves and have little fear of them. The black male, on the other hand, is strong and has nothing to lose, because he has nothing. There are no jobs available for the majority of them and majority women know this. They also know black men are tired of their position in society and are full of rage. Most majority women, not yet knowledgeable about the truth concerning black men, still want to enjoy their comforts, so they live in fear and ignore the plight of black men.

Black men are also a majority woman's fantasy. She has been told all her life not to become sexually involved with black men. This is considered forbidden fruit for them. All adults know that the very thing parents restricted them from, became their primary obsession when growing into the teenage and adult years. Black men and majority women are becoming more and more sexually acquainted today. Myths about black men are slowly crumbling because of their contact with white women.

Majority males are afraid of black men. They too know what has been done to Blacks and guilt plus shame causes them to fear them. J.A. Roger's point was well made in "Sex and Race", Volume III:

> ...the race question is so ridiculous that it makes one look silly even to take notice of it. For instance, even as the elephant is afraid of the mouse we find in America that nine-tenths of the nation with the army, the navy, the political machinery, and nearly all the wealth gives the appearance of being afraid of the feeble one-tenth, the Negro.[5]

> "European males have always had the propensity to say 'I feel threatened' while holding a gun to somebody else's head."[7]

Majority males continue to try to dominate black men out of fear (law enforcement), control of resources (economics-no, or low paying jobs) and psychological and physical self destruction. There are more black men in jails in this country than any other race in America. Brutal law enforcement officers herd them into courts where they are sentenced to extreme jail terms. Many of them are murdered on the streets by trigger happy policemen who more often than not get away with murder.

Many majority men also have penis envy. They are of a group not known to be very well endowed. This is a well known fact as noted by J.A. Rogers in "Sex and Race" Volume III, when Alex Hrdlicka of the Smithsonian Institution was quoted as saying:

> The penis (of the Negro boy) is longer than that of the corresponding white boy.[8]

He also quotes Sir Harry Johnston in, "British Central Africa" as saying:

> In both sexes the development of the external sexual organs is large-larger

than in the European (white) race, more considerable than among the Mongoloid yellow race of Asia, America and the Pacific.[9]

Mr. Rogers also quoted Havelock Ellis from his "Studies in the Psychology of Sex":

> I am informed that the sexual power of Negroes and slower ejaculation are the cause of the favor with which they are viewed by some white women of strong sexual passions in America and by many prostitutes. At one time there was a special house in New York City to which white women resorted for these "buck lovers". The women came heavily veiled and would inspect the penises of the men before making the selection.[10]

White men see black men as sexual beings they fear white women will prefer if everything were equal in this country and intermarriage the norm. They strive to keep black men out of touching distance of their wives, sisters and daughters (a hypocritical stance, since their pursuit of black women has been tenacious). Their motivation to "achieve" is energized by the need to maintain distance from the two things they fear the most; black men and poverty. They owe black men an astronomical sum (forty acres and a mule with interest) which they are not ready, nor intend to pay. If such payments were forthcoming, (the sum is so huge) black men would surpass them in every treasured area of their existence. If they were aware how often many majority married and unmarried women entertain minority men sexually (not just black), they would be horrifyingly surprised. Minority women are aware, because many majority women seek them out, usually at work, to confide in them. Majority women cannot tell other majority women about these rendezvous because of possible betrayal, so they confide in women they assume will not have contact with their community. Some of them pursue black men because they are knowledgeable of their husband's trysts with black prostitutes, or lovers.

Black men are the last to be considered for employment. Media attacks on them causes fear within the populace leaving them to create their own society within society to stimulate cash flow (drugs).

Without college educations, they are left with menial jobs paying minimum wages which are not adequate to support their families. College educated black men are also finding it more and more difficult to obtain employment. Drugs and guns are being sold in black communities at a rate beyond that in overall society (by ratio). Where do the guns come from? Black people do not manufacture them. Drugs are emptied into black communities by the tons. Black people do not import them either. This is an organized operation to provide the tools for black-on-black destruction. Black men's rage must have an outlet. Dominant forces within society want to see that rage self destruct.

Individual racism is personal. Every person of color reaching adulthood has experienced some form of racism if they have had contact with Whites. The simple act of shopping for groceries can be stressful. To wait at the checkout counter with a few majority individuals in front of you getting the "Hi, how are you doing today?" greeting from the white cashier checker, and you step up to "Are you paying in stamps or cash?" This is insulting and painful. You know the checkers have been trained to greet each customer the same, but there's something about the color of your skin that causes white checkers to drop their voice into a cold resonance and readily assume you're on public assistance. You hope the people standing behind you do not notice your embarrassment as you move on. This is a normal reaction Blacks receive in this society. It seems as though majority people want Blacks to remain uncomfortable. This state of being is "unnatural" for anyone, especially if encountered on a daily basis throughout the years. Rage builds and begins to fester at such a seething rate that a great many Blacks try not to place themselves into positions to encounter Whites. Let's look at this from another angle. When a person awakens in the morning, they prepare for the day. They will wash, shave, or put on makeup. While looking in the mirror, they are not seeing color. They see themselves. It's much like walking around during the course of the day. They are not conscious of their own skin color. They are operating from an inner world devoid of superficial considerations. So now they leave home, and enter the marketplace. They may stop at a local 7-11 for a newspaper, and on the way in, hold the door open for a majority person behind them out of common courtesy. The person says nothing, and gives them a dirty look. Immediately they are reminded of what color they are. It makes no difference whether the majority person sneered at them out of racial hatred or not. The constancy of majority hostility towards them throughout the years, automatically plunges their psyche into the inner sea of rage.

Fine restaurants are the same way. A black couple entering can't help but notice all eyes scrutinizing them with hostility. The couples first reaction may be to leave, but since this has happened so often in the past, they ignore other patrons and wait to be seated. Whites are actually saying to them, "we don't want your kind here" and the black couple knows it. Their unspoken reaction is "Tough, we're staying. We have as much right being here as you". No matter where Blacks go in this country, the same reaction is experienced. One would wonder where the strength comes from to endure this atmosphere of hate and repulsion. Since it is a fact of life, it is as normal to Blacks as breathing. This does not mean they accept it. They look at people doing this as so-called "superior inferiors". That is, people who consider themselves superior, yet, exhibit inferior behaviors.

Majority people do not understand how Blacks pick up on the signals white people send each other when Blacks are around. The answer is simple. Any person of color can walk into an environment and tune into the "vibes". They can't help it. It's an automatic response due to the melanin in their skin. Sensations are stronger than those Whites experience, that is why they cannot and do not understand, nor believe it. It is beyond their comprehension. This must be a reality because most majority people think their messages are clandestine, and fly over the heads of the victims. It is more advantageous for Blacks to sense, ignore, and proceed with the business at hand. They know Whites are looking for stereotypical reactions from them, and refuse to comply. Sometimes the rage is so deep, it only takes a spark to light the fuse, and there are quite a few sparks out there. An example of black rage at it's worse is clearly defined in "Native Son" by Richard Wright.

Much that has been exposed here will raise eyebrows and cause much dissonance. This is expected along with challenges concerning information given. When truth is exposed to the light of day, those opposing it will fight desperately to qualify their actions, reasoning and purposes for concealing it. Now their actions are laid bare, reasoning proven unsound, and purposes revealed (economic).

V

UNDERSTANDING BLACK CULTURE

Black culture is varietal in its universal scope. It is a dish with many different African spices; American, West Indian, Spanish, African, and other contributors from many Third World countries. They all add to the essence of the rich African flavor that has transformed religion, style of dress, and life styles of all Americans.

Let's start off by saying, there are no pure races on this planet we call "Earth". All evidence points to "African Eve" being the mother of all homosapiens. The most significant evidence is the tracing of blood types back to their origins. If we assume this to be so, all people came from Africa and migrated to other lands for agricultural purposes, glacial melting, tribal conflicts and other unidentifiable reasons. As these people moved away from their ancestral lands, climates changed. The wide nose was no longer needed to breathe comfortably the farther north they traveled away from the equatorial sun. The hair also changed for no longer was it needed to deflect hot rays of radiation beaming down upon it. Melanin was lost for the same reason. This process may have taken many hundreds, or even thousands of years. There is still evidence in the most ancient of countries that Africans were the first people to trod upon the soil.

There are Indians in Asia as black as most Africans. They are called the Dravidians (descendants of the first Africans to inhabit the area). They still wear African garb, and if the customs, art and beliefs of Asian Indians are carefully studied, African influence can be seen throughout. Indian women wear their jewelry in the same ways as African women (around the heads, arms, wrists, and ankles, in ears and noses.

In the orient, Africans left their art in the form of statues and large stone heads. They all have African features as well as the Buddhas of old (some had their hair corn-rowed). The original Chinese and Japanese were called Negritos. Read, *"Sex and Race" Volume I* by J.A. Rogers.

The European migrators (the Grimaldis) entered a very cold area where they were more than likely the first migrators to show real signs of physical change due to the dramatic change in climate. The Moors raided throughout Europe much later, impacting on the customs, music and ethnicity of the inhabitants.

Throughout history, people have miscegenated without thought to color. Color became important later when it became economically profitable to enslave people to obtain free labor, but their use had to be explained. Since Africans did not speak the language, They were thought by European people to be unintelligent. They were declared less than human, therefore, paving the way for abuse and misuse of them.

All of the above migrants do not claim immediate ties to Africa, and have preferred to establish their own ethnic and national identities. Recent (within the past 800 years) African migrants and former slaves retain their cultural ties and beliefs. West Indian traditions also reflect strong African roots.

During the slave trade, Africans were first taken to the Caribbean where they were shipped out to their final destinations. Some of these ports of call were:

Area of Importation	Number of Slaves (1451-1870)
Brazil	3,646,800
British Caribbean	1,665,000
French Caribbean	1,571,900
Spanish American (Caribbean, Mexico, Central and South America)	1,552,000
Dutch Caribbean	500,000
Britist North America (U.S. and Canada)	427,300
Danish Caribbean	28,000
Old World (Europe, Atlantic Islands)	175,000
Total number of slaves	9,566,000

(From The Atlantic Slave Trade: A Census, by Philip Curtin, Madison University of Wisconsin Press, 1969.) [1]

Slaves brought to America suffered miserably. They were chained, beaten, fed poorly and sold to Whites. The majority of them were taken to plantations where they suffered even greater cruelties under brutal masters. Some were lucky to be placed with kind masters (masters more compassionate than the former). Over three centuries of hostile, demeaning servitude did not completely assimilate the African into American society. They still held on to their music, and identity with a place "across the water". Today, assimilation has taken place to a greater extent. The need to grow and participate in the "American Way of Life" has driven many to dive into untested waters. Moving forward and upward has been slow and unsteady. During their climb, many have suffered death, defeat, loss and dreams deferred. Few have been rewarded, martyred, deemed great and regarded as role models or leaders. Through it all, very few have given up their identity and culture (no one knows how many have and are passing for white).

The ever effusive nature of black folk touches the soul. Their laughter comes from a place thirsting too long for joy, and when it comes, bursts forth like a billowing flood. They dance to a drummer heard only through the ears of a tortuous past forcing them to bounce, move, sway, jump, twist, turn, bodies doing any and everything their spirit commands. Songs sang from the depths of a soul captured, lost, devoid of spirit, renewed and vibrant. They stride searching for surefootedness with a rhythmic movement toward a hopeful goal. Their hand-slapping, foot-tapping rhythm and gaiety beguiles those not familiar with enjoying life. The smooth, suave demeanor surfacing when discernment is needed, confuses those expecting the buffoon. Natural mother wit perplexes the extremely educated still attempting to know and understand life. The giving natures happily sharing half of the next-to-nothing they have. The down-to-earth "being for real" quality the educated ones possess that is not expected by those looking for "European-like" behavior. And last but not least, the ever latent "mask" needed for protection. Black folk are beautiful in all ways. There is no greater joy experienced than being around a group of black people having fun. They feel the music, sense your sorrow or joy, and with twinkling eyes soothe your soul.

Their culture is filled with natural things. Innate memories surface in the gold youth seems obsessed with, for their fore-fathers and mothers adorned themselves elegantly. The earth is their touchstone. Concrete and paved sidewalks takes them out of nature and forces them into a world of cold hard surfaces. Breathing air and being in touch with the elements are what they want and need. Being with people, energizes them. To touch is to communicate. That is the way of black folks. Let them come together and hugs abound, hand slapping and bussing causes auras to connect making them feel alive. They need love ever so much, so this is their way of expressing it to each other to counteract the hostility in the environment. They have so much love to give, yet, it is rebuked as "happy-go-lucky". They are warm people with the genes of a warm/hot climate surging through their, beings. They have withstood everything raw and terrible that can be done to human beings and they are still able to smile. Isn't that incredible?

Slaves placed on plantations in the islands (Caribbean)

miscegenated with native Indians and Whites. White masters bred black concubines (like their English cousins in America), consequently producing mulattos, quadroons and octoroons. The slaves never relinguished customs brought from their native land. They too have that effervescent quality about them. Their music captivates them into dances normal to their African forefathers. Their women carry bundles upon their heads as their great, great great grandmothers in African villages did daily. Although European and Indian influences broadened their customs, their impact on the Caribbean has been more profound, especially their religious and holistic practices of self healing. The West Indian's migration to America in the past 80 years (in large numbers) has added diversity to black culture in this country. Music has been injected with the reggae beat, dread locks (symbol of freedom) have created a new fashion statement, and a flood of information about their struggle has begun to permeate black communities.

Puerto Rican populations have also added their spice to black culture in America. Their story is basically the same as the West Indian's. They derive from the mixture of African, Indian and Spanish (viceroys conquered Puerto Rico). Their colors range from white to black. Many of them deny their African heritage since coming to America, but they cannot deny the African influence in their music. Their dances also prove the African connection. Their dance movements are African. The ability they exhibit in performing their dance movements has to come from within. These kind of movements can't be imitated, they must be inborn. Research in Puerto Rico proved instrumental in finding the African in them. Travels throughout the rural areas unearthed black Puerto Ricans. Most were older and seemed hidden away. Questioning of them proved fruitful. Younger, lighter-skinned relatives were sent to larger towns to obtain employment at white businesses that rejected the dark parent or parents. In America, many of them miscegenate with Blacks more so because of white racism towards them than a sense of relatedness.

Native American Indians cannot be left out of the miscegenation process. They mixed more with Blacks than Whites as has been noted in a report by the Secretary of War when regarding the

Massachusetts Indians in 1822:

Very few of them are of unmixed blood, the number of pure Indians is very small, say fifty or sixty, and is rapidly decreasing. The mixture of blood arises far more frequently from connection with Negroes than with white.[2]

In 1849, the following was said in a report of the commissioners relating to Indian affairs in Massachusetts, No. 46:

There are about six or eight Indians of pure blood in the state. All the rest are of mixed blood, mostly Negro.[3]

The Virginia Bureau of Vital Statistics no longer recognizes any Indians in that state but classes them all as Negroes. In 1924, two college professors, working under the Carnegie Institution, made a study of the Virginia "Indians," particularly the Wins and decided that they were largely Negro and mulatto.[4]

In lower New York State, especially on Long Island the Indian had largely vanished into the Negro by 1800. Prime, writing in 1840, says that among the Shinnecock and the Montauk Indians, "not more than one family" could boast of aboriginal blood but had "similarly amalgamated with African blood." He adds, "By mingling with the African race whose condition in this country is even more depressed than their own, they have degraded instead of elevating their condition in the eyes of the community and stamped an infrangible seal on their condition...

For many years there has been a growing jealousy of their claim to the lands reserved by their ancestors and an evident desire to see it extinguish. And it is common to hear that 'these mongrel people' have no more right to these lands than the aborigines, or Africa. "It must indeed be confessed if the Indian title was based on purity of aboriginal blood it is already extinct for want of a claimant. But the circumstance that the Indians have seen fit to ally themselves in marriage with those of a darker hue can furnish no just excuse for disfranchising and disinheriting their legitimate posterity."[5]

Throughout the United States Indians and Blacks were drawn to each other, both being targets of white persecution and oppression.

Present day migrating Africans have infused black Americans with a more realistic view of the Motherland. They have brought tales of life-styles (destroying Edgar Rice Burroughs mythical Tarzan scenario), history, village life, values and traditions. Most of them seek not one, but two, three, four, five and sometimes six college degrees. Most of them are highly intelligent and have amazed many Blacks with their dignity and demeanors. Since exposure to them, black Americans have defined themselves more from the Afrocentric point of view than American.

Black people are a spectrum of many races intertwined; the foundation of them all is African. Only the most spiritual, physically sturdy, and mentally capable people could withstand what they have had to endure. Their culture reflects beauty, strength, courage, hope, creativity and a natural ability to adapt. Children should be immersed in it to appreciate what it is that makes them who they are.

Religion has been the root of all black endeavors since ancient times. The very soul of black folk basks within spirituality. In Africa, men, women and children rejoiced in dance and song to the Creator. This has not changed. Black churches resound with joyful praise, dance and song. Western religion was thought (by the oppressor) to calm and sedate the African soul, to "civilize" and "reculturalize" them. Black folk took religion and breathed life into it according to God's mandate (Bible: "Make a joyful noise unto the Lord, all ye lands"). All of their pain, hate, suffering and joy came out thunderously within the confines of their churches and homes. The spirit would grip their bodies, taking them to a place where no man could harm or reach them. The same spirit was taking hold of the African descendants in Haiti, South America, the West Indies and Puerto Rico. Although called by other names, the gods were the same. They had to express themselves in the way their natures dictated to show their love and devotion to God. Mesmerized with the spirit, they all strutted, threw their hands up and shouted while praising the Gods of Africa that did not forsake them, but rather embraced them in alien places that were horrible and cruel. Majority people cannot understand the commitment of black people to retain the need for self expression. They do not know who the African is. They do not know, nor understand the depths of a relationship with the Creator that has spanned all time, and what is not understood is vilified. They consider black expression as "idolatry and heathenistic behavior."

Black churches are becoming more "Africanized". New awareness has given rise to new churches practicing the Yoruba, MAAT, Ausar Auset (Ancient Egyptian religion of Isis and Osiris) Islam, and many other religions. The services are accented with African instruments blending together into a rhythmic percussion above which songs of African freedom and glory of God ring out. Children, dressed in African garb, pound proudly upon drums with innate correctness in tempo with their heartbeats. Adults shake, flay, push, and pull various sized instruments adding melody that flows gently above the hypnotic, tantalizingly exotic syncopation. Everyone is involved. Unified voices sing out as bodies move and spirits soar. Complete beings (bodies, minds, spirits and emotions) profess to the heavens, their all. After praise, quiet sermons devised to instruct correct living are provided, along with study periods and discussions. Each group has its own format for services. The thing to note here is the way all black people express themselves no matter what religion they practice (this does not include "Europeanized" Blacks practicing Western-type religions that require "quiet" reverence).

Dr. Clarence Walker speaks of the way black women worship in his sermon, "Restoring The Queen Within: Black Women in Prophecy":

> There is a spiritual beauty that African-American women have that is unique. What is it? You know how to love the King (God). There are times when God is wanting that from you. He's looking down from Heaven saying, 'you know how to praise me. You know how to worship me. You know how to reverence me.' God said, "If you do these things, I will greatly desire your spiritual beauty."[6]

Most Blacks are serious about reclaiming their heritage. A prime example would be the African garb now being worn in churches, to work, during leisure, and when attending events (majority and ethnic). The styles are free flowing and colorful. Most dresses and suits are tailored to fit American life-styles and are acceptable at all occasions. Kente cloths add great touches to tuxedos and suits on men and women. Not only does the wearing of African garb give one the feeling of belonging and pride, it also supports black entrepreneurs s striving to survive. They have given Blacks an alternative to "European" dress that has pizzazz and dignity.

Children's garb can be made by parents, or bought in African stores across the country. Woman's garb are dresses, Abijans (A-bee-john), full dresses with crowns, Bubus (Boo-boos) (skirts and blouses, or dresses are available with embroidery around the neck and shoulders), wrap skirts, Iro (ear-row) and blouses, Bubas (boo-bas).

Men's garb are flat top round hats Felas (fee-las), (can be worn by men and women), and Kufis (Arabic for Muslims) (koo-fees) pants sets. These are just some of the names of outfits available to those looking to change their mode of dress.[7]

African dress is quickly becoming the norm among the black populace. It means more than just a new look, it's a new attitude. It's an attitude of connectedness. The need to identify with something outside the realm of "whiteness" and taking on someone else's culture. Black people are beginning to see the beauty in their own roots. The truth has been lying dormant for too long, and when it surfaced, it came like a mighty wind to engulf the ignorant and forlorn. No longer are black people "children lost in the desert of ignorance". With truth comes light, courage, understanding, rebirth and a second wind to boost the spirits.

Kwanzaa

Kwanzaa is an American holiday that pays tribute to the rich cultural roots of Americans of African ancestry. Kwanzaa means "the first" or "the first of the harvest", in the East African language of Kiswahili. It is observed from December 26th through January 1st. Kwanzaa was founded in 1966 by Dr. Maulana Karenga, a Black Studies professor who describes himself as a cultural nationalist. Kwanzaa originated as a cultural idea and an expression of the nationalist US organization which was headed by Dr. Karenga. Kwanzaa is unique in that it is neither a religious, political, nor heroic holiday but rather a cultural one. Gifts may be exchanged during Kwanzaa though it is suggested that they not be given if they present undue hardship. When gifts are given it is suggested that they be creative i.e. handmade or functional like a book. To celebrate Kwanzaa, a table should be prepared with the following items:

Mkeka: A place mat usually made of straw.
Kinara: A candle holder for seven candles.
Mishumaa saba: Seven candles.
Mazao: A variety of fruit.
Vibunzi: Ears of corn representing the number of children in the home.
Zawadi: Gifts.
Kikombe cha umoja: A unity or communal cup for pouring and sharing libation.

Each day of Kwanzaa, a candle should be lit beginning with the black candle which is placed in the center of the candle holder. Candles are then lit alternately from left to right. Three green candles should be placed on the left and three red candles should be placed on the right. Each day a principle should be recited when the candle is lit. The importance that each principle has for the person reciting it should be expounded upon.

Kwanzaa's Seven Fundamental Principles of Nguzo Saba.

1. **Umoja= Unity:** To strive for and maintain unity in the family, community, nation and race.
2. **Kujichagulia= Self determination:** To define ourselves instead of being defined, named, created for, and spoken for by others.
3. **Ujima= Collective Work and Responsibility:** To build and maintain our community together and make our sister's and brother's problems our problems and to solve them together.
4. **Ujamma= Cooperative Economics:** To build and maintain our own stores, shops and other businesses and to profit from them together.
5. **Nia= Purpose:** To make our collective vocation, the building and

Morgan State University Presents

Jeanette Davis-Adeshote'
author of
Black Survival in White America: From Past History to the Next Century
Friday, February 24, 1995
11:00 am
McKeldin Center

About the Author

Born Jeanette Davis in Harlem, New York, Ms. Adeshote' experienced racism at an early age. As a result of this, she has spent most of her professional life in the study of the African-American experience. An inquisitive visit to the Egyptian Museum in East Berlin was the catalyst for the book, *Black Survival in White America: From Past History to the Next Century.*

In 1989, Ms. Adeshote' graduated Summa Cum Laude with a Bachelor of Science in Broadcast Journalism from Morgan State University, where she also worked as an on-air personality and music director for the campus radio station, WEAA. Her play, "Grandma Loved Roses," won Baltimore's WMAR-TV's Drama Competiton for Black Writers and was televised in 1985 featuring Baltimore's Arena Players.

Ms. Adeshote' has spent over 25 years gathering data, traveling to verify origins of African peoples and delving into Africa's splendid agelessness.

Program
Ms. Trista Hargrove, Presiding

Greetings
Dr. Allan Kennedy,
Professor of Telecommunications,
Morgan State University

Introduction of Guest
Ms. Trisch Smith
Speaker

Presentation
Ms. Jeanette Davis-Adeshote,*writer*
Black Survival in White America:
From Past History to the Next Century

Question and Answer Session

Closing
Ms. Trista Hargrove

*Thanks to All Those Who
Assisted with This Program*

developing of our community in order to restore our people to their traditional greatness.

6. **Kuumba= Creativity:** To do always as much as we can, in the way we can, in order to leave our community more beautiful and beneficial than when we inherited it.

7. **Imani= Faith:** To believe with all our heart in our people, our leaders and the righteousness and victory of our struggle.

(Dr. Maulana Karenga Sept. 7, 1965)

Black culture (mixed as it is) has evolved into African Reclamation. All peoples of recent African descent are reclaiming what was lost but not denied (whites would not let them deny it by constantly reminding Blacks of who they were and are). This has turned into a blessing in disguise. If Blacks were permitted equality in all European societies at the end of slavery, there would be more assimilation into the mainstream of the Americas, British, Dutch, Portuguese, Danish, Spanish, French, and European life. Since this has not happened, they were and are forced to look "from whence they came" in order to make sense out of their existence and place in God's plan. God is making good his promise to the lost tribes of Israel (Europeans) if his commandments are not met in Deuteronomy 28:43-44 and 62-63:

43. The stranger that is within thee shall get up above thee very high; and thou shalt come down very low.

44. He shall lend to thee, and thou shalt not lend to him: he shall be the head, and thou shalt be the tail.

62. And ye shall be left few in number, whereas ye were as the stars of heaven for multitude; because thou wouldest not obey the voice of the Lord thy God.

63. And it shall come to pass, that as the Lord rejoiced over you to do you good, and to multiply you; so the Lord will rejoice over you to destroy you, and to bring you to nought; and ye shall be plucked from off the land whither thou goest to possess it.

As the year 2000 nears, the white population is depleting. All efforts to increase its numbers are failing. Minorities are growing at a tremendous rate (Hispanics, Asians and others more so than Blacks due to governmental immigration practices keeping black foreigners out of the United States-Haitians). It is no accident that black culture is being renewed at this time. Black people are being prepared to regain that which is lost. The signs are evident in all segments of society and the world. Europeans are being removed from power in places colonized for centuries. South Africa was the last pocket of colonialism. Black rule there will dispel all majority efforts to portray Blacks as incompetent leaders. Because of these changes, black people will have to revamp their thinking. Dependence on others will have to end. The need and time for self-determination is not coming, it is here.

Retaining and restoring black culture on a higher level is a necessity. By never having lost faith in God, black people are being blessed to witness a new day with the nightmarish horrors behind them. They must be forever vigil for change will not come easily to those hoping to retain and regain that which will be inevitably lost. By never having lost faith in themselves, black people can be proud of their survivability amidst insurmountable odds. By returning to their roots, black people will find solutions to racist, sexist and international problems that abound today.

The root of the matter is wisdom. Trial and hardship have honed a people into psychological "beings" receptive to change, and ready for spiritual and emotional leadership of a nation. The "prodigal" has awakened and stands ready for the call. Although many will stand as one, two times the number will fall by the wayside. Those having allowed themselves to be swallowed up by temptation to life destructive forces, will deplete in large numbers, and the sick will clean up or self-destruct. This is to be expected. However horrific, the failures must be accepted as well as the victories. A major victory is needed now to give purpose and reason to black peoples sojourn in the Americas. A weakening power structure will present the scenario for such a victory to take place.

The loosening grasp upon the throats of Third World nations by the power brokers, stems from the brokers loss of economic control rather than human rights commitments. Their attention is drawn to their purses, for the thief of time-in-one-place-too-long (Capitalism), has left greed running rampant throughout the populace rightly demanding larger pieces of the economic pie. Devaluing whole nations of people is the plan in operation today within the most powerful countries in the world.

By lowering living standards in the United States, government can better control the resources of a country running out of control. People are killing each other wild west style, taxes are not being paid by too many individuals and businesses, schools have deteriorated, drugs abound, vigilantism is on the rise, health care systems have failed to serve as designed, state and federal agencies have evolved into bureaucratic paradises for those controlling them, and the beat goes on.

The present generation of youth is the "interim" generation. The next generation will grow up within an atmosphere where the accepted wage will be $5 to $8 dollars an hour, and slightly higher for High School graduates. No more will union songs be heard, because unions will no longer exist. The older generation of workers who fought for fairness, job safety, protected wages, bargaining rights, and many of the taken for granted benefits provided by employers, have begun to check the pulse of their beloved unions. Employee solidarity of purpose has eroded, and with them the benefits employers were forced to provide.

So now, "Atlas" has "Shrugged", causing high wages, low taxes, low inflation, low-cost health care, and governmental and state regulations to fall by the wayside. The unmanageable will eventually become manageable as excess among the masses is slimmed down. The diet will continue for many many generations to come. Once control has been attained, it would be unwise to let it again become uncontrollable.

Knowledge has to be applied with wisdom for anything or any people to become successful in their endeavors. Studying all aspects of the world they live in along with environmental factors impacting on their existences are crucial. Knowledge of decisions being made and how they affect the lives of all people, and having the power as well as the voice to create positive change are key.

Black people have uncanny perceptions of what will work because they are first-hand observers of all the mistakes made by their captives.

Africans, African-Europeans and others with black strains from, J.A. Rogers, "Sex and Race" Volume I:

Charlotte Sophia-Queen of England, Consort of George III, and great-great-grandmother of George VI
Ludwig Van Beethoven-Composer
Honorius-Roman Emperor
Septimus Severus-Roman Emperor
Hannibal-General
Henry III, Emperor of the Roman Empire (1017-56 A.D.)
John VI, King of Portugal
Alessandro Dei Medici, Duke of Florence
Gustavus IV Adolphus, King of Sweden
Queen Sophia of Sweden
Alexander Dumas-Writer-"The Three Musketeers"
Robert Browning-Poet
Pushkin-Father of Russian Literature
Murat-King of Naples
Macrinus-Emperor
Firmus-Emperor

(Rogers): Volume III:

Thomas Tallis-The Father of English Cathedral Music
Kamehameha the Great King of Hawaii
Kamehameha II-King of Hawaii
King Kalakaua-Hawaii
Queen Liliuokalani-Hawaii
King Lunalilo-Hawaii
Balthasar-one of the Three Wise Men
His Highness, Syed Alwi, Rajahof Perlis, Malaya
Bernardino Rivadavia-First President of Argentina-Mulatto

VI

MOVING TOWARD THE YEAR 2000

The year 2000 is the turning point for Blacks around the world. It signals a new beginning that calls for preparation and dedication on the part of those aspiring to participate and contribute in the changing of America.

There's a great need for black doctors in black communities. According to Andrew Hacker ("Two Nations"), there has been a decrease of 1.4% physicians since 1960. This means the quality of black health is being trusted to majority physicians. This also means wealth that could be retained in black hands is being pocketed by white males, white women and Asians. Bright students should be encouraged to enter medicine in order to contribute to the longevity of Blacks. Medical researchers are also needed. Genetic diseases such as sickle cell need to be researched. Since this disease is commonly found in Blacks, black researchers would have a vested interest in finding a cure.

Black College Professors are also declining by .5%, says Hacker. There is a great need within universities throughout the country (white and black). It is no secret that white colleges and universities are not apt to employ black instructors, if so, it is usually to satisfy governmental requirements for loans or subsidies. Many black academicians have gone into other fields due to difficulty finding employment.

White colleges should be challenged on the grounds that black representation by instructors should be in parity with the percentage of black students. With the rising minority population, it would be in their best interest to hire black professors now. Past experience has proven that institutions will most probably have to be forced to change their way of doing business.

Since there is a large percentage of Blacks overrepresented in prisons in this country, black lawyers are needed to assure Blacks fair representation. According to Hacker's figures, Blacks are underrepresented in law to a great extent. Black lawyers are direly needed because they are more prone to understand the societal circumstances, and the justice system. Black lawyers can also act as gate-keepers assuring black clients that the justice they receive is fair, and all attempts have been made to protect their rights.

Journalism is a field dominated by majority persons who are unwilling to allow many Blacks to enter the field. Thousands of black journalism majors have given up after years of trying to enter the field. Friends, and friends of friends are placed into vacant slots in newsrooms, television stations and in print media. Personnel offices do not handle media placements. Positions are acquired by who you know and what influence a powerful relative might have. This locks Blacks out unless a "token" slot is available, or something spectacular happens. Blacks holding positions today are fortunate and know it. Their advice is usually, "keep trying, and you can also do great things". This is not so, and statistics prove it. One of the greatest under represented professions for Blacks is journalism, says Hacker. This does not mean that the doors locking Blacks out should not be knocked down. Blacks should be encouraged to continue to strive in this area. It wouldn't hurt to ask Blacks in the field for assistance. If they are truly dedicated to black advancement, they will.

Black owned radio and television stations are available around the country. They should be approached for employment by aspiring broadcasters. Not only do black stations service the community, most of them are committed to supporting newcomers. Of course, there are always a few interested in just making money with no thought of bettering the communities they operate in. Stay clear of them for they serve no purpose other than to serve self. Listening to stations is a sure way of determining their commitment.

Entrepreneurs are needed in all areas of the economy. Black communities have been known to have Jews and Asians servicing them in neighborhood stores. This practice is still the norm, but, a change is in the wind. In Jewish neighborhoods, Jews service the community. In Asian neighborhoods, Asians service the community. In black communities, Blacks should service the community. This can be achieved by the pooling of resources by people in black communities, family foundation loans, and opening black banks for Blacks to secure loans. Many black entrepreneurs are not waiting for large amounts of money to open businesses. They are obtaining vendor licenses and selling on the streets of large cities across the country. This is a way to parlay funds for future self-investment.

The necessity for self determination is crucial now. Frederick Douglass stated how important it was in his time and it still holds true today.

Our destiny is largely in our own hands. If we find, we shall have to seek. If we succeed in the race of life it must be by our own energies, and by our own exertions. Others may clear the road, but we must go forward, or be left behind in the race for life. If we remain poor and dependent, the riches of other men will not avail us. If we are ignorant, the intelligence of other men will do but little for us. If we are foolish, the wisdom of other men will not guide us. If we are wasteful of time and money, the economy of other men will only make our destitution the more disgraceful and hurtful.

He who starts behind in the great race of life must forever remain behind or run faster than the man in front.
Benjamin E. Mays.

The greatest black under-representation are in the following occupational fields, according to Hacker:

Waiters & Waitresses	4.7%
Editors & Reporters	3.8%

Bartenders	3.6%
Engineers	3.6%
Lawyers	3.2%
Physicians	3.0%
Realtors	3.0%
Photographers	2.9%
Speech Therapists	2.8%
Biologists	2.7%
Designers	2.6%
Dental Hygienists	2.5%
Architects	0.9% [1]

American Blacks need to start importing and exporting African and American goods to be sold in this country and abroad. Black people are starved for things "African", and Africans need American goods. This could become very lucrative now as well as in the future. One trip to Africa would prove beneficial in creating business ties and opportunities. This market will be cornered, so why shouldn't Blacks be the ones in control of it. African countries are always looking for financial input to aid in the growth of their economy, and surely black Americans can use the cash flow. There is no need for large cash outlays. This type of business can start small and escalate in time. If wealthy Blacks decide to partake in such a venture, they can with relative ease. This would definitely be a wise investment. There are enough stores available to sell African garb, books and figurines.

At this moment, then, the Negroes must begin to do the very thing which they have been taught that they cannot do. They still have some money, and they have needs to supply. They must begin immediately to pool their earnings and organize industries to participate in supplying social and economic demands. If the Negroes are to remain forever removed from the producing atmosphere, and the present discrimination continues, there will be nothing left for them to do.
Carter G. Woodson.

With economic growths declining within European and American economies, there is fear within majority people. We know well what this kind of fear can do. We also know how non-productive races have been dealt with in the past because of economic down turns. Hitler introduced methods still studied by majority scientists today.

While black college enrollment has spiraled upward through the years, upon completion, few companies are willing to employ them. More black businesses are needed to employ their own. Self determination and black advancement go hand in hand. This does not mean white applicants should not be hired. It simply means black businesses must now concentrate on providing employment for Blacks at a higher percentage. White businesses are for the most part "lily white". They do not hire Blacks unless their hiring poses an advantage of some sort (economical). In fact, white employers have "buzz words" for private employment agencies they employ to find employees. A few "buzz words" used are: "All American" (blue-eyed, blond haired), "Ivy-leagued" (same), or "A-1" (white). These games played by white employers are illegal and discriminatory. When black job seekers fill out applications, they are welcomed only to satisfy Equal Employment Opportunity laws. If they have applied, employers can erroneously say the applicants have been granted interviews, but were not qualified for the positions. Since these companies are determined not to open their doors, Blacks need to build their own doors to open to future Blacks seeking advancement.

Affirmative Action is another area that presents irritation to majority people.

With their numbers dwindling, Whites cannot see the need for minorities filling the gaps that will be left by them in the future. They are concerned with the here and now. They feel Blacks are taking jobs they, by simply being born white, are entitled to. They do not care about injustices done to Blacks for over 400 years. They could care less if Blacks have not been allowed to equally participate in Mainstream America, until recently. They want what is due them because they are so-called "superior" and deserve the "best" this country has to offer.

Black thinking is just the reverse. In the past Blacks were

denied equal opportunities. Many whites migrating to America forgot that Blacks were already here working for little or no wages. Black investment in the country has been and is so astronomical that it cannot be estimated. The work of slaves created jobs for Whites as they migrated to the colonies. The cotton was picked, ginned, and sent north to factories where white workers ran the machinery. They made their livelihood off the backs of Blacks. This they could not and cannot see. Today, it would be chaotic if laws were not enacted to permit minorities to share a piece of the economic pie. Since laws have been enacted, enforcement of them has been slow and painful. Blacks have not gotten anything free. Everything has been paid for in blood, loss of lives, and hostile persecution. Affirmative Action just allows upward mobility into areas previously closed to minorities. Although many of these doors still remain closed, efforts are underway to change behaviors to bring businesses into compliance with the law.

Minorities differ in their perceptions of their relationships with each other and with Whites within the American "melting pot". While Blacks, Asians and Hispanics feel they have been limited, Whites seem to think they have ample chances to succeed:

In one of the most comprehensive statistical portraits to date of minority views toward whites and toward one another, the survey found that, while the nation's three largest minority groups believe their opportunities are limited by racial perceptions, whites believe minorities have ample opportunities.

"It's as though white America is sleepwalking on the edge of a volcano of ethnic and racial differences," said Sanford Cloud Jr., president of the National Conference (formerly the National Conference of Christians and Jews), which commissioned the survey.

It found that 80 percent of Blacks, 60 percent of Latinos and 57 percent of Asian Americans surveyed felt that their groups did not have opportunities equal to those of whites. But among white respondents, 63 percent said Blacks have equal employment opportunity, 57 percent said the same of Latinos and 63 percent said it of Asians.

"In a nutshell," Cloud said, "We have two very different views of opportunity in America...and the gap that's represented by those views has got to be closed."

The survey, released in a climate of heavy media coverage of racial tensions, reported that members of minority groups are more likely than whites to hold negative stereotypes about other minority groups, including religious minorities such as Jews and Muslims.

For instance, 33 percent of latinos, 22 percent of Asians and 12 percent of whites surveyed agreed with the statement, "Even if given a chance, (African Americans) aren't capable of getting ahead."

On Jews, 54 percent of Blacks, 43 percent of Latinos, 35 percent of Asians and 27 percent of non-Jewish whites agreed with the statement, "When it comes to choosing between people and money, Jews will choose money."

At the same time, large majorities of survey respondents believe that Blacks "have made valuable contributions to American society" and "will work hard when given a chance." And 59 percent of non-Jews believe that Jews "are charitable and supportive of social justice for others."

The most surprising element in the survey is the perception of how each group viewed the other:

The Ford and Joyce Foundation surveyed 2,755 respondents nationwide, including 1,000 Blacks, 502 Latinos and 154 Asians.

Asked whether whites "are insensitive to other people and have a long history of bigotry and prejudice, "66 percent of the minority respondents said yes, including 76 percent of Blacks, 56 percent of Latinos and 54 percent of Asians.

The survey also found that, contrary to popular belief, a majority of whites support affirmative action programs in hiring and promotion. By a 55 to 31 percent margin, white respondents endorsed such programs. Black respondents supported affirmative action by 71 percent to 20 percent, Latinos by 64 to 20 percent and Asians by 57 to 30 percent.

While all groups in the survey embraced the importance of cultural diversity in society and education, one set of questions produced an ironic series of results:

"Whites feel most in common with African Americans, but least in common with Asian Americans. African Americans feel most in common with Latinos and least in common with whites and Asian Americans. Latinos feel most in common with whites and least with African Americans. Asian Americans feel most in common with whites, who feel least in common with them."

Still, members of each group said they were willing to work with those with whom they have the least in common. [2]

(Washington Post, March 3, 1994)

Because of Affirmative Action, many Blacks have advanced which brings Blacks closer to being in parity percentage-wise with whites. Still, there is a long way to go. Majority people have been in a race for over 400 years. Blacks have just left the starting gate. How long will it take Blacks to catch up? That is really the question that should be asked of whites disagreeing with Affirmative Action. The fact that Blacks have been patient for so long is amazing. They have compromised with legislators to make it as fair for whites as possible, yet, whites being used to having "it all", do not want to comply. In the future it will pay off for everyone. Just as everyone has to sacrifice for deficit reduction, it would have been commendable if whites had agreed to do the same to bring Blacks in parity with them in the 60s. Maybe by now Affirmative Action would be less needed. If not Affirmative Action, what would whites deem fair?

Reparations have been paid to the Japanese for the time spent in camps during World War II. Blacks have been incarcerated in America for over 400 years and have not been recompensed. Even when Marcus Garvey encouraged Blacks to return to Africa, he was silenced because the government refused to allow Blacks to leave. After emancipation of slaves took place, a move to transport Blacks to Africa by former slaves, racists and abolitionist whites was thwarted by sabotage. They were not allowed to leave. The purpose in keeping Blacks in America was for cheap labor, not love. Now the drive is on for payment to Blacks for the free and cheap labor performed by their forefathers and mothers. What would it take to repay them? Would $2,000,000 dollars per person be enough. Is that the fair escalating payment for 40 acres and a mule with interest? Would the government be willing to pay $90,000,000 to rid itself of the black problem? Taxes Blacks pay would more than cover that. Would $2,000,000 dollars apiece place Blacks in parity with whites? If Blacks were given the money, how long would it take for white and black vultures (white collar businessmen and women) to swindle if from them (those incapable of handling large sums of money). Or, would it be adequate to cancel the payment of taxes for Blacks for 100 years, or the number of years enslaved? This is something that has to be mulled over, and negotiated by Blacks in conjunction with the American government. More programs will not work. Past thefts by program administrators and their staffs proves money never reaches the ones it was intended for. How about land? Would that solve the problem, or escalate the hostile relationship between Blacks and Whites, and does it matter? What is the solution? One thing is certain. Blacks will have to be compensated. It's not a matter of if, but rather, when and how.

America owes to my people some of the dividends. She can afford to pay, and she must pay. I shall make them understand that there is a debt to the Negro people which they never can repay. At least, then, they must make amends.
Sojourner Truth.

Your country? How came [sic] it yours? Before the pilgrims landed here we were here. Here we have brought our three gifts and mingled them with yours: a gift of story and song -- soft, stirring melody in an ill-harmonized and unmelodious land; the gift of sweat and brawn to beat back the wilderness, conquer the soil, and lay the foundations of this vast economic empire two hundred years earlier than your weak hands could have done it; and the third, a gift of the spirit. Our song, our toil, our cheer, and warning have been given to this nation in blood-brotherhood. Are these gifts worth the giving? Would America have been America without her Negro people?
W.E.B. Du Bois.

Welfare has a strangle-hold on the progress of all black people. As long as some Blacks are stalemated, there will always be negative impacts on all Blacks. Welfare should be phased out to allow all Blacks a chance for upward mobility. Blacks fortunate enough to be "distanced" from food stamps, Medicaid and monthly hand outs, are needed desperately by those still locked into the system. The fortunate ones could take one welfare family and show them how the system (American economic system, governmental bureaucracy, and job market) works. A little time spent each week mentoring will have a tremendous affect upon welfare recipients wanting to change their lives, but do not possess the knowledge to do so.

Governmental bodies need to set limits on how long individuals can receive welfare. If five years was to be the limitation period, this would allow enough time for vocational, or formal education to be completed (time must be allowed for problems that may arise during this process). After five years, all benefits are cut off. Individuals receiving incomes at, or up to 3% above the poverty line should receive benefits for child care and Medicaid until their income increases beyond 3% of the poverty line. This would enable welfare recipients to get a foothold secure enough to keep them anchored in the work force.

These people should be trained in areas that have future potential for growth. Vocational schools offering training in areas destined to phase out, or become obsolete (their main objective is securing government funds), should not be sanctioned by governmental agencies. If this war against poverty is going to be won, it has to be attacked from an intelligent, well planned, market-wise perspective. The old way of doing business has not worked efficiently. This battle is not being fought for Blacks alone, but for all unfortunate peoples who should be given equal opportunities in their "pursuit of happiness and prosperity."

There is always the need for black legislators. The purpose of having representation in Congress and the Senate is to assure our voices are heard. Black communities across America need to continue sending eligible Blacks to Washington. No matter what obstacles they face, they must be supported with enthusiasm. If they are found to be inadequate, others should be voted in to work diligently for the people and not him, or herself. Once this is understood, they will have greater impact on the system. They also need to have more contact with their constituents year round, not just in election years. They should update their constituents on what is going on that will alter or enhance their (constituents) lives. In the past, many representatives have become mesmerized with power, and become swelled with self-importance. They must know they are there by the grace of the people, not theirs, and there is much work to be done for the growth and survival of "the people."

Blacks have been successful in many areas of entertainment. Music has proven to be very lucrative for Blacks. Many have started their own record labels and are now producing black talent. The motion picture industry leaves much to be done. It has not yet gotten the message that there are black stories to be told. Alex Haley's success should send a message, but whites haven't gotten it yet. Very few mini-series have gotten as many viewers (black and white) as "Roots", "Roots-2nd Generation" and "Queen". Black writers and screen writers are hungry for avenues to present their stories on film. It would help if wealthy Blacks saw the advantage of pooling resources to purchase a major motion picture studio. Banks would loan them the money, because they have collateral to back it up. The black populace would support such a venture, if well advertised, to prove a venture such as this can be successful. Some doors need to be built when others are impenetrable.

Never should black folk forget those who entertained our minds and souls when oppression's tight grip had us gasping and grasping for freedom. God has not forgotten us. When he smiled upon us, Maya Angelou came forth, majestic, regal, and dignified tripping words off of tongue as if birthing them into life anew. Nikki; fiery, yet, gently reminding, scolding and lovingly soothing the soul of black folk into action. What of Langston? Can't you hear him pounding out verse to drum, pushing deferred dreams into fruition? Cool, jazzy Bird, transcending and soaring the spirit to untamed heights? Oh yes, Mahalia, sing to us of joy, love and heavenly praise. The velvety sounds of Nat, enchanting us with unforgettable melodies of love. How about Bessie singing those low down dirty blues? The "A" train didn't leave the station until Duke got there. Can you hear the voice of an angel? That's Marian enthralling the world with her "once in a hundred years voice". Satchmo "cooked" and Handy "grooved" while Bojangles moved to the "tap dance" beat.

> Zora Neale knew we were a "cracked plate",
> then Countee Cullen came to set us straight.
> But who can forget Nina with her "heart beat",
> And Lorraine's "Raisin' " had us all on our feet.

Mom's Mabley made us laugh through tears,
and when we were sad, Pigmeat and Skillet were here.
And how about Pryor, satire and all,
and then came Murphy, he's having a ball.
God gave us Aretha to caress our souls,
and Carmen McRae? She broke the mold.
There's no one like black folk with spirits so sweet,
and they're still steppin' to Mother Africa's beat.

"Soul food" is an intricate part of back culture. The term has often meant; pork chops, pig ears, pigtails, pig feet, fried chicken, collard greens, mustard greens, turnip greens, candied yams, corn bread, chitterlings, hog maws and other dishes high in fats and cholesterol. This suicidal binge needs to change, These same dishes (except pork) can be prepared in a healthy manner (cooking methods will be suggested later). As the year 2000 nears, good nutrition is a must.

The dishes above were cheap survival dishes during slavery and after the emancipation. Nutrition was not a factor to Blacks. To eat period was a blessing. Today, eating habits need to be redefined for survival's sake, High blood pressure , cancer and heart disease have become epidemic among Blacks mostly due to poor dietary habits. Black babies are dying of malnutrition because their teenage mothers do not know how to properly feed them. Proper nutrition should be taught on a higher level than now taught in schools, and to the public at large. The four major food groups can kill anyone if basic knowledge of how they should be prepared, how much should be consumed, and the purpose each contributes to bodily functions is absent.

Dairy products (animal products) are high in fats and cholesterol (milk, cheese, butter, eggs). They should not be consumed on a daily basis. Labels should be checked for low salt, low cholesterol, and low fat brands.

Bread can be very high in fats. To avoid problems, eat wheat

breads and rolls. And if a spread has to be eaten, a low fat, no cholesterol margarine can be as tasty as butter once gotten used to.

Poultry and fish are excellent meal favorites as long as they are
not cooked in saturated fats. Vegetable oils, used sparingly, can be
used if frying is preferred. Baking cuts down the need for oils, and is
the most nutritional method.

Pork should not be consumed. But, since it is difficult for some
people to give up, it should be cooked the same as poultry and fish
making sure it is well done before it is eaten.

The killer is red meat. If at all possible, refrain from eating any
type of red meat. If it must be consumed, eat small portions either
baked, broiled, or micro-waved. Meats may be high in proteins, but
they are also high in saturated fats that fill the fat cells of the body
causing an abnormal body structure and obesity, plus this fat is the
hardest to lose. Many over-weight black men and women can't understand why they gain and retain weight when they have been eating
the same way all their lives. That is the problem. They have been
eating incorrectly all of their lives, and as their metabolism slows
down in the later years, they no longer burn off the fat, therefore it
fills the cells and creates more fat cells to fill. Layer after layer of fat
cells accumulate until the organs become overloaded with the strain
of supporting the body, and cease to function. This is called, death.

Parents are guilty of telling children to eat their vegetables, but
do they tell them why? In most cases, parents fall short on information that their children can benefit from for a lifetime of holistic health.

Vegetables and fruits aid in digestion and each has a unique
quality. Carlson Wade and Dale Koppel in "Wonder Foods and Juices",
explains just how unique they are:

Asparagus-contains asparagine, an alkaloid that helps stimulate the kidneys to break down fat and improve circulation. When
alkaloids are distributed throughout your body, they have a direct impact on your adipose cells and flush out fat.

Beets-promote a diuretic washing action via your liver and kidneys because of their unique low-level iron content. It cleanses blood cells and washes away fatty deposits. Beets also contain natural chlorine to help wash away fat in your liver, kidneys and gall bladder.

Cabbage-Cabbage contains valuable properties that cleanse your system of waste. Red cabbage is especially high in fiber. Cabbage has a very high sulphur and iron content. These minerals serve as cleansing agents for your stomach and gastrointestinal tract. They also cleanse the mucous membranes and wash out fatty deposits.

Carrots-are a prime source of beta-carotene which is converted by your digestive system into usable vitamin A, which accelerates your metabolism. Carrots are also a good source of potassium, virtually fat free and high in soluble fiber. Raw, they are a source of vitamin C.

Onions-contain natural volatile oils and minerals that control fatty build-up. They keep blood in great shape by thinning it, retarding clotting, lowering total cholesterol, and regulating sugar. Onions have also been known to kill bacteria, relieve bronchial congestion and reduce allergies.

Radishes-contain high concentrations of iron and magnesium, which dissolve fat, wash it away and establish the proper liquid environment needed for healthy tissues.

Tomatoes-rich in vitamin C and natural citric acids, speed up the metabolism. They also have a concentration of lycopene, a type of carotene which is an anti-cancer agent. Tomatoes are low in sodium (salt) and fat and rich in potassium.

Cucumbers-contain a great deal of sulphur and silicon which stimulate the kidneys to wash out a dangerous waste product, uric acid. When the acid is washed out, cellular fat is loosened and swept away.

Brussel Sprouts- are beneficial in the fight against cancer, especially of the colon and stomach.

Apricots-one of the few fruits that have enough beta-carotene to flush out fats and wastes. For maximum results, eat fully ripe apricots.

Bananas-contain a number of nutrients that help stabilize your gastrointestinal region. They help wash away fatty wastes from your kidneys and other vital organs and are great energy boosters.

Cherries-cleanse away wastes that otherwise cause irritation. They are high in iron and are an excellent laxative, blood builder, and gallbladder and liver cleanser.

Grapes-have been known to prevent tooth decay. They can inactivate viruses, and studies have shown that they are rich in cancer-blocking compounds.[3]

These are but a few of the many fruits and vegetables that are available to cure what ails you. But wait, there's more!

Fiber is essential. "Fiber scrubs away fatty deposits in your cells", says Wade and Kopple, and they indicate the six prime sources:

Whole Grains-wheat germ and unprocessed bran are ideal sources of cell flushing fiber.

Vegetables-they should be eaten raw whenever possible or cook them only enough to make them palatable.

Tuberous root vegetables-this group includes carrots, parsnips, white and sweet potatoes, turnips and kohlrabi. Their skins are especially high in fiber, but even if you peel them, you still have a high-fiber food.

Fruits and vegetables with tough skins-those that contain edible seeds are especially beneficial. They include all varieties of berries, tomatoes, squash and eggplant.

Pod vegetables and legumes-these include green beans, green peas, dried beans and peas, lentils and lima beans. Be careful not to overcook them. As soon as they are tender enough to be palatable, they're ready.

Seeds and nuts-use both shelled and un-shelled varieties. Avoid any that are salted. Be sure to chew seeds and nuts thoroughly.[4]

Investigate the secrets of the foods you are putting into your body as you move you and your family toward the 21st century in good mental, physical, emotional and spiritual health. And remember, **SUGAR, SALT, TOBACCO AND ALCOHOL HAVE NO NUTRITIONAL VALUE!**

VII

THE SOUL OF BLACK WOMEN

Prior to slavery, black men placed black women above them selves in respect and esteem. Children born to her were identified by her bloodline, not his. Within black communities today, her innate ability to take control has diminished the black man's "European" evaluation of himself.

The concept of women being of divine essence reaches back into ancient times as noted by Ivan Van Sertima (relating to modules found among ancient Black of Egypt, India and the Sinai Peninsula):

> The fact that women as spiritual beings were considered full partners in civilization-building was reflected historically in Egyptian society by records kept on women-pharaohs and indicated a widespread belief that women also housed the Divine. Moreover, the first version held that women were the repositories of civilization, the keepers of the secrets of society, the mothers of gods, the manifestations of a universal "feminine" principle which saw the universe, the earth and subconscious as a "womb" for the expression of Divine will.[1]

Another version was also developing, according to Van Sertima:

> ...one which considered man primarily a material entity, whose happiness was measured by his ability to acquire and maintain a material heaven (wealth and pleasure).

In that heaven, women were not principals that predicated or participated in social policy, but were objects of sensuality or objects to be used by men. Moreover, it was held that women were to be kept from principal positions because they would be luxuries acquired by men and they would not have the strength to protect the accumulation of material wealth.

The materialist theory held that the material heaven was the basis of man's paradise and that women, as weaker members of that paradise, were to be objects of and not participants in the building of that material paradise. It might be interesting to note here that the materialist theory of civilization did not deny the divine element. It simply conscripted the Divine and placed it in the service of the materialist aim.[2]

Examples of the first version is Akkenaton (Akhnaton) and Nefertiti, Isis (the original black Madonna, according to Van Sertima) and Osiris, Queen Ahmose-Nefertare (who ruled with her husband Ahmose), Ahotep (the mother of Ahmose who ruled with her husband King Seqenere Tao II, and after his death). Van Sertima uses an eighteenth Dynasty inscription to describe her rule:

The King's wife, the noble lady, who knew everything
Assembled Kemet. She looked after what her Sovereign
Had established. She guarded it.
She assembled her fugitives.
She brought together her deserters.
She pacified her upper Egyptians.
She subdued her rebels,
The King's wife Ahotep given life.[3]

No book could be written about ancient African Queens without mentioning Nubian Queen Tiye. Again, Van Sertima tells us of a woman beloved by all. She lived from 1415-1340 B.C. and was co-regent (ruler), Great Royal spouse of Amenhotep III, and mother of Pharaoh Tutankhamen and Akhenaten. Her husband said of her:

The Princess, the most praised, the lady of grace, sweet in her love, who fills the palace with her beauty, the Regent of the North and South, the Great Wife of the King who loves her, the lady of both lands, Tiye.[4]

The names go on and on of great black women in antiquity taking the helms of nations and ruling them with great dignity and wisdom.

As indicated in an earlier chapter, black women in Africa (especially in Islamic Sudan), were treated as gifts from Allah. The greatest of respect was given them, and no man owned them. They did not give up their belief of women being divine when embracing Islam. When women spoke, everyone heeded their counsel. They existed within a society built on truth, justice and fairness.

The second version is what plagues today's society. It began to flourish when Arabs, Greeks and Romans began to invade Africa raping her of her wealth and legacy.

All women were soon relegated to the position of sensual objects of ownership. Men being of superior physical strength, could easily subdue them. Laws were soon enacted making it legal for men to whip, jail, and even kill their wives if caught in acts of adultery. Women had no rights at all.

Black women withstood continuous invasions of their bodies by whites. It seemed as though whites were intoxicated with Mother Africa's daughters, mesmerized to the extent of needing to have them near them whether in slavery, as contemporary lovers, or making occasional visits to brothels where accommodating black women were and are available. From this connection phrases like, "once you go black, you can't go back" arose. It has been the custom for black men to steer clear of white women (taboo), but it has never been taboo for white men to pursue black women. White women wish it to be verboten, but this has just added spice to the clandestine means in which white men seek to satisfy their dusky hungers.

The heavy burdens placed upon the black woman during slavery never destroyed her spirit, perseverance, or determination to survive, and protect her family. When black men were held at bay, she pushed forward any way she could to assure some modicum of advancement. If it meant letting the master have her body (he could never have her love, soul and spirit-which he is still trying to master), she would let him do so. If it meant nursing his babies because his lazy wife didn't want to destroy her youthful breasts, she relented. If it meant washing floors and scrubbing toilets so her children could go to college, nothing was beneath her. If it meant being treated horribly while cleaning racist white women's houses, she endured. If it meant putting her dreams aside in order to advance the race, it was no big thing. If it meant giving her life for the struggle, she never hesitated. When black men sold their votes when they finally were able to vote, she fought for the right. When black men were being lynched, she was the one responsible for the passing of a no lynching law. When doors would not open, she pleaded, begged and knocked them down for the "brother's" and "sisters" to walk through, and she is not Divine? She doesn't need a throne, because she doesn't believe in useless pedestals anyway. She has enough sense to know that in today's society, the treating of women as second class citizens is the norm, and a throne is just a pretty seat to sit upon. She always knew deep within her soul that her ability to lead and rule was and is natural to her. She doesn't think about it, she just does it. Read, *"When and Where I Enter: The Impact of Black Women on Race and Sex in America",* by Paula Giddings.

If black men are to ever understand black women, they must first understand the history of who THEY are. They were great rulers who had no fear of women. They enjoyed the minds, hearts, souls, bodies and beauty of women. They adored, respected, bejeweled, and honored them. They ruled beside them and trusted them to rule well in their absence. They walked as equals upon the earth. Their children respected them and honored them. They were united in their efforts, and were of one mind. This was a union that could not be defeated by outsiders. This is the type of union that is needed today.

The male model held up by the establishment to be emulated, is the powerful male being in charge of a family comprised of a wife and children. He is the breadwinner and protector. His wife is presumed weak, and his children dependent upon him for their survival. This is quite interesting, because most families today are not nuclear families. Anyway, black men have fallen into ill repair by using the same yardstick for themselves as white men use in this regard.

Black men falter in that they feel they should be in control of their women and families, when in essence they should work with them to achieve collective goals and dreams. If the woman is allowed to make upward mobility, the man should work with her until such a time comes when she can assist him, or he can make headway on his own. He shouldn't deter her growth and advancement because he is not in control of it. The reality is, he is not. To live with that may be difficult, but what else is there? White men have created a world that works to their advantage. The same world does not aid the black man in his aspirations unless his aspirations are "to be just like his captors". The two cultures are opposite sides of a coin and should be dealt with accordingly. If Blacks do not have a different agenda than what is being exhibited today, what is the struggle all about? If Blacks were in charge tomorrow, would there be an end to racism and sexism? Would racism no longer be acceptable, but sexism is? Where are we going, and what is the agenda? There has to be unity between black men and women in order to institute meaningful change for all people be they male and female, or of diverse hues.

Since black men have been held at the bottom of the social and economic realm because they are considered to be the strength of the race, they hunger more than anyone else for a chance to succeed and move forward for they have yet to savor collective success. The first step in achieving this is to rid black neighborhoods of distractions that deter growth. Liquor stores and posters need to be taken away by those who wish to gain capital from the same communities their products are destroying. Suburban areas do not tolerate these advertisements, or stores in their areas at such a volume. Cigarette advertisements need to be outlawed in black communities. Black men of character and strength need to make themselves available to youth and other black men who are lost due to hopelessness and are more prone to imbibe and use drugs. Techniques of survival have to be taught within this society that provides many weapons of destruction, most of which require assistance from the victims. Maybe if people knew they were paying the companies to kill them, maybe they would be less prone to overindulge in cigarettes and alcohol.

Next, churches could play a larger role in opening up their doors to provide youth with alternate activities outside of religious ones. After-school centers in churches could provide a place for children to go watch meaningful videos, do homework, play games, conduct study groups (on their history), and teenage sensitivity group discussions. This would keep young black boys and girls out of harm's way in the streets and enable them to become educated about themselves and each other.

There are many productive black men in American society. They need to make their voices known within the communities of America. They are the silent group America seldom hears from. Their silence does not assure survival (unseen so nonexistent). Their input is needed and would be welcomed to help steer today's black youth in the right direction. A few black men have opened youth centers in various cities, while others are working with young black boys in schools for black boys only.

Black men are needed to rise now and stand with black women to create meaningful change. They have spewed forth a few great men, but now we need the majority of them to join in the struggle for the healing of a nation within a nation suffering from self-inflicted wounds psychologically designed by a long standing adversary.

The soul of black women thirst for the mist of love's nectar so long withheld in the desert of America's repulsiveness. Her guardian and mate, lost within himself, cannot give to her that which can deliver her from her deprivations. She must suffer in silent hopes of easing his pain in order to glean some iota of love. She must look past his insensitivities in order to touch a part of him locked away from everyone, even her.

The soul of black women strives toward the unknown, knowing innately that she will arrive in a place designed for her alone. A place no one can move her from. She relentlessly trudges on, generation after generation, not caring so much that she may not be the one to arrive for someone must pave the way.

The soul of black women thrives on challenge and is generated by love and tenderness. With her haughtiness as armor and her "attitude" as fortification, she stands tall with giants while casting spells upon her adversaries not ready for her ebonic ebulliency.

The soul of black women cry out in despair in the dark of night for love. Must it be neglected a lifetime? When will it come? Her man tied, bound by ties of mind and spirit too strong for her to break. She must move along through the valley of the shadow of death with the tempestuous fever of love beating within her breast going unassuaged. Love excites her. It moves her. Love stimulates her very being. Sex only gratifies, but **love,** it quickens her very existence and everything she has to bear is worth a few moments in its grasp. But for now, black women are "Lovin' On Next To Nothin' ", as Gladys Knight and the Pips so aptly put it.

THE SOUL OF BLACK WOMEN

When I look in the mirror,
I see eyes of Black old women,
young women, and girl babies

A look of knowing the pain,
joy, and strength of just
being human

They possess the loins of
ancient Candacian Queens
battling to assure their existence

Their blackness is in God's image
for the Creator's delight

They are clothed in mysteries never known
to anyone but them
They feel my pain from their own
experiences

Above it all, we know each other
well-- it's in the eyes

My sisters somewhere inside themselves
know the plan
They innately sense when patience
is a strategy, when action
a must

Through the eyes in my mirror,
dreams are moving into fruition
dreams of "doin' what I want to now"

Hathor, the Great Mother of all
woman am I
I am she who taught the earth it
could give birth
From my deepest sensual being came
Kings and Queens

From my mind, I give strength to a
people
Raising them up from ignorance to
reasonable thought

I have flowered the world with beauty
from the blackest to total loss of
melanin

I kissed the Sun with prayers of love,
and I planted human seed astutely
I have been wise in choices, until rape
change the plan

Still I move stealthily doing as I
must for the survival of all

These eyes have seen Osiris, and Horus
is a familiar sight

Men seek dark mysteries in my
sensuality

They search in primitive places for
contemporary answers
While my mind has all they seek

Home to Mother Africa
My heart thrives to the tempo
of the drumbeat

Back to the inner "knowing"
Back to the promise made long
ago as I kissed her earth upon
my uprooting

Back to who I am, why I am
and forever will be

Without me, the earth would grow pale
and unfeeling
The rivers would cloud in need of my
prayers

The tempestuous souls of "The People"
would lose faith
Without me, Life would be a void and
Unvarietized

I AM A MUST

When I look in the mirror
I see the body of Isis
Black as coal I stand
The blacker, the silkier to the touch

My sleekness is as a stallion in the wild
Moving like a lynx, purring when content
naturally loving until pained

There was a time I anointed my
body with precious oils
enjoyed ornaments of gold upon my
velvety skin

To touch my skin is to journey into the
deepest abyss of the origin of womanhood
My mirror empowers me with vivid vision
of what I possess

My body reflects ultimate resentment to
unnatural allegations of inferior being

My mirror shows me knees unable to bend
in the mind

My tongue is sore from containment
My feet spread wide for the journey
are ridiculed

My hair is uniquely mine
They provide tools for its destruction
I will not comply

My full succulent lips are worshipped
They want them too, but pale shall not
have this reward naturally

My cheekbones are proud, structured
as finely chiseled stone, unrelenting
and firm

My breasts stand out proudly
expressing their fullness of purpose
My back is strong to bear the burden

My spirituality is who I am
It sculptured my physique for
survival in a desert of ignorance
to self

The drum is my heartbeat
Sister Nina told me that
It's in her eyes too
The sister who's just like me

I still stand tall within the Creator's
bosom
For I came from the first mold of humankind
I am the mother of all
The original creation that mankind wishes
to deny

But only through me can mankind validate itself
for
I AM AFRICAN EVE

VIII

BLACK HEROES

GREAT BLACK MALE HEROES: SUNG AND UNSUNG

Robert S. Abbott: Founder and builder of the Chicago Defender (Newspaper)

Ira Aldridge: Opera Singer, "The greatest of all Othellos"

Muhammad Ali (Cassius Clay): Three time World heavyweight boxing champion -- The Greatest

Richard Allen: Founder, Bethel African Methodist Church

Arthur Ashe: 1st black male tennis champion

Machado de Assis: First great writer of Brazil

Harry Belafonte: Actor, Singer and Activist

Dr. Jesse McDade Bey: Philosophy Professor - Morgan State University

Ralph J. Bunche: Professor, Writer, Diplomat and Nobel Peace Prize winner

Roy Campanella: One of the first Blacks to play on a major League Baseball Team

Frederick Douglass: Anti-slavery spokesman and publisher of "The North Star"

W.E.B. DuBois: Activist, Leader of the Niagara Movement and writer

General Alexandre Dumas: ("Alexandre the Greatest"), Commander of Napolean's Calvalry

Alexandre Dumas, Fils: Re-maker of the Modern French Stage

Alexandre Dumas, Pere: The World's Greatest Romancer

Paul Lawrence Dunbar: Afro-America's first great poet

Issac Fisher: Educator and noted prize-winning Essayist

Carlos Gomes: First Great Operatic Composer of the New World

Matthew Alexander Henson: First man to stand on top of the world (North Pole)

Michael Jackson: "Superstar" Breathed life into the record industry, and became its biggest record seller

Edward A. Johnson: Historian, College Professor, 1st Negro member of the New York Legislature

Jack Johnson: World heavyweight boxing champion

Michael "Air" Jordan: One of, if not the greatest basketball player of all time

Ernest Everett Just: Pioneer in Biology

Joe Louis: World heavyweight boxing champion, from June 22, 1937, to March 1, 1949

Nat Love: aka, "Deadwood Dick" - Cowboy

Thurgood Marshall: Supreme Court Justice / Won "Brown vs. Board of Education" decision as a young lawyer

The Honorable Kweisi Mfume: Former City Councilman (Baltimore, Md.) Presently Congressman and Chairman of Congressional Black Caucus

Benedict the Moor: Saint of the Catholic Church

Bill Pickett: aka, "Ducty Demon" - Cowboy

Adam Clayton Powell: New York Congressman

Aleksander Sergeevich Pushkin: Father of Russian Literature

Paul Robeson: Actor, Singer, Rhodes Scholar

Smokey Robinson: Singer and songwriter

Jackie Robinson: 1st Black Major League baseball player

Charles Clinton Spaulding: Financial genius and insurance magnate

Henry Ossawa Tanner: Modern painter of religious subjects

William T. Vernon: Bishop of the African Methodist Episcopal Church, College President, and former Register of the United States Treasury

Paul R. Williams: Architect

Carter G. Woodson: Pioneer in Negro History and Education

GREAT BLACK FEMALE HEROES: SUNG AND UNSUNG

Marian Anderson: Singer

Joyce Antoine: School Administration/Union representative - Newark, N.J.

Yaa Asantewa: "Great Queen" of Ghana (fought against the British)

Isabella Ashby: Beautician (32 years), Community Activist and supporter and provider of elderly care for the indigent

Pearl Bailey: Singer, Actress, U.S. Diplomat to the United Nations

Ida B. Wells Barnett: School teacher, writer, lecturer, organizer and leader of the Anti-lynching campaign

Louise Beavers: Actress

Makeda Belkus, aka, Queen of Sheba: 960 B.C. She ruled Axum, Arabia and Ethiopia

Mary McLeod Bethune: First black woman appointed as director of the Negro Division of the National Youth Administration by President Franklin D. Roosevelt, June 24, 1936, educator and founder of Bethune Cookman College

Jane Mathilda Bolin: First black woman judge of the Domestic Relations Court of New York City. Appointed July 22, 1939

Carol Moseley Braun: (of Chicago) On November 3, 1993, became the first Black female Senator

Gwendolyn Brooks: First black poetry Pulitzer Prize winner. Her book "Annie Allen" won in 1950

Shirley Chisholm: First Black female Congresswoman, "A Catalyst for Change"

Cleopatra: Queen of Egypt. Ruled Egypt from 51 B.C. - ?

Alice Coachman: First black woman to win a gold medal in the 1948 Summer Olympics (London, England) high jump competition

Rebecca Lee Crumpler: First black female medical degree recipient - Boston's New England Female Medical College, March 1, 1864

Dorothy Dandridge: First female black best actress Academy Award nominee for, "Carmen Jones"

Rita Dove: In 1993, became the first black female appointed as United States Poet Laureate

Crystal Bird Fauset: First black woman in a state legislature (Pennsylvania House of Representatives)

Elvira Ford: Public School Administrator (Virginia)

Aretha Franklin: The "Queen of Soul"

Althea Gibson: The only black woman to win Wimbledon singles tennis competition, in 1957 and 1958

Mother Hale: Founder of Hale House for care of infants with Aids

Fannie Lou Hamer: Field Secretary for SNCC, organizer (Mississippi Freedom Democratic Party) and spokeswoman

Lorraine Hansberry: Playwright. First black female to have her work performed on Broadway stage

Hapshepsut: 1505-1485 B.C. First warrior Queen in African history. Ruler of Egypt for 21 years

Barbara Harris: The Episcopal Church's first female bishop

Marcelite Jordon Harris: First black female U.S. Air Force general and wing commander

Patricia Roberts Harris: First black woman head of a U.S. embassy

Dr. Lucia Hawthorne: Professor of speech, Morgan State University

Elizabeth Ross Haynes: Domestic Service Secretary of the United States Employment Service

Dorothy Height: President, Council of Negro Women

Anita Hill: Lawyer and Professor. Spoke before Senate Investigating Committee on her sexual harassment charges against proposed appointee to the Supreme Court, Clarence Thomas

Zora Neale Hurston: Writer

Dr. Mae C. Jemison: On September 12, 1992, became the first Black woman astronaut to travel in space on the Space Shuttle Endeavor

Hazel Winifred Johnson: First black female Brigadier general, and the first black chief of the Army Nurse Corps

Queen Dahlia-al Kahina: Mauritania, 688-705

Leontine T.C. Kelly: First black female bishop of a church (United Methodist Church, San Francisco)

Jackie Joyner Kersee: First woman to win two gold medals in Heptathlon competition

Eartha Kitt: Singer, Actress and Activist

Queen Latifah: "Rap-Her" on the female side and actress

Glenda Lewis: Psychiatric Nurse, Irvington, New Jersey

Louise Marie: Illegitimate daughter of Queen Marie-Theresa, wife of the King of France, Louis XIV, became known as the Black Nun of Moret

Moms Mabley: Comedienne extraordinaire

Arenia Cornelia Mallory: President of Saints Junior College, "The Biggest Little School in the World", in Lexington, Mississippi

Hattie McDaniel: First black, male or female to win an Academy Award. Best supporting actress for, "Gone With The Wind"

Toni Morrison: In 1993, became the first black Nobel Prize winner for literature

Constance Motley: First black woman Borough President (New York City). Also first black female U.S. District Court Judge

Nzingha: Queen of Angola from 1623 to 1659. She led an army against Portuguese intruding forces

Rosa Parks: Seamstress. Refusal to give up a seat on a local bus gave rise to the Montgomery Bus Boycott

Mary Jane Patterson: First black female B.A. recipient, Oberlin College-1862

Tamara Primas: Director of Gloucester County Education and Training Administration (JTPA), Woodbury, New Jersey

Charlotte E. Ray: First black female lawyer in the District of Columbia, April, 1872

Ida Gray Nelson Rollins: In 1887 became the first black female dentist, University of Michigan Dental School

Dr. Eunice Yvette Rudisel: Gynecologist, North Carolina

Diana Sands: Actress

Nina Simone: Songstress with a "heartbeat"

Mary Church Terrell: First black woman appointed to Wash-

ington, D.C's. Board of Education
Queen Tiye: Nubian Queen of Egypt,1415-1340 B.C. Mother of Tutankhamen. Ruled with her husband, Amenhotep III
Harriet Tubman: (Moses) Led slaves through underground railroad to freedom
Sojourner Truth: Itinerant and Activist
Cicely Tyson: Actress extradordinaire
Madam C.J. Walker: First (modern) black millionairess
Ethel Waters: Singer and Actress
Phyllis Peters Wheatley: First black to become published, (poems on various subjects, religious and moral) in 1773. Her work was in great demand by whites and blacks alike
Nancy Wilson: Songstress extraordinaire
Oprah Winfrey: The most popular talk show hostess in the world
Debbie Wright: Television Newscaster

Little Known Facts*

The Grimaldi, a Negro race, lived in Europe as late as 12,000 years ago. Two complete Grimaldi skeletons are in the Museum of Monaco, near Monte Carlo. Abundant traces of their culture have been unearthed in Southern and Central Europe.

The Negro was the first artist. The oldest drawings and carvings yet discovered were executed by the Negro peoples over 15,000 years ago in Southern France, Northern Spain, Palestine, South Africa and India. The drawings are on rocks, the carvings on bones, basalt and ivory.

Cheops, a Negro, built the Great Pyramid, one of the Seven Wonders of the Ancient World. It is 451 feet high, has 2,500,000 blocks of granite, each two and a half tons, covers 13 acres, took 100,000 men thirty years to build and was completed in 3730 B.C.

Negroes lived in America thousands of years before Columbus.

Central American monuments show numerous carvings of them as gods. When Columbus came to the New World, Negroes had been crossing from Africa to South America a distance of 1600 miles. The first white men to reach the American mainland, tell of seeing Negroes. Columbus who visited South America said that he heard of them there.

Beethoven, the world's greatest musician, was without a doubt a dark mulatto. He was called "The Black Spaniard." His teacher, the immortal Joseph Haydin, who wrote the music for the former Austrian National Anthem, was colored, too.

Jan Ernest Matzeliger, a Dutch West Indian Negro living in Lynn, Mass., invented the first machine for sewing the soles of shoes to the uppers. This invention, which was eleven years in the making, revolutionized the industry and gave shoe supremacy to the United States. It made several millionaires, one of whom left $4,000,000 to Howard University. Overwork and privation hastened Matzeliger to his grave in 1889 at the age of 37. He left a few shares of stock to a white church, which later saved it from being sold for debt.

The Mohammedans believe that Moses was a black man. Their Bible, The Koran, says so. God told Moses to put his hand into his bosom. The Koran says that it came out white. The commentators declare that Moses hand could not have been white before, and that the miracle Jehovah intended was making the black skin white, and then turning it black again. The Septaugint, or Greek Bible, agrees with the Koran.

The characters of the Bible are largely Negroes. The Jews were slaves to the Egyptians for nearly 430 years. Only seventy Jews went to Egypt with Jacob. The Bible says that 600,000 men left with Moses, which according to Haushoffer, meant a total of 3,154,00 with women and children. For this large number to have left mixing with the Egyptians, who were black, must have taken place on a vast scale. About 12,000,000 Negroes were brought to the New World. Imagine how much of their original color and culture the latter would take with them should they return to Africa, and you realize how much of the original Jew remained in those seventy Jews after four centuries. Tacitus, Roman historian of 90 A.D., says that the Romans of his day popularly believed that the Jews, which then abounded in Europe, came from Ethiopia, the land of the Blacks. The present white color of the European and American Jew, is very likely due to the same cause, as the fair skin and straight hair of large numbers of Negroes. The Bible classes the Ethiopian and the Jew together, "Are ye not as the children of Ethiopia unto me, O children of Israel, saith the Lord." Chaldea, the land in which the Jews originated, was also a Negro land, hence Abraham might also have been black.

The Falashas, or Negro Jews of Ethiopia, led by Queen Judith, put the line of Solomon and the Queen of Sheba off the throne of Ethiopia in 937 A.D., and they ruled for forty years. The Falashas assert that they are the original Jews. They call themselves "The Beta-Israel", or "The Chosen People."

Imhotep of ancient Egypt, was the real Father of Medicine. He lived about 2300 B.C. Greece and Rome received their knowledge of medicine from him. In Rome he was worshipped as the Prince of Peace in the form of a black man. His Ethiopian portraits show him a Negro. Imhotep was also a Prime Minister to King Zoser as well as the foremost architect of his time. The saying, "Eat, drink, and be merry for tomorrow we die," has been traced to him. Hippocrates, the so-called "Father of Medicine" live 2,000 years after Imhotep.

The oldest and most noted statue in the world bears the face of a Negro. It is the Sphinx of Gizeh, which was worshipped as Horus, or Harmachis, the Sun-God of light and life. It was erected about 5,000 B.C.

The devil which is now depicted as black, was once portrayed as white. When the black man dominated the planet he painted the forces of evil, white. When the whites came into power, they shifted the colors. But as late as 1500 the Ethiopians still depicted their Gods and heroes black and their devils and villains white. Father Fernandez, a Catholic missionary, who worked amongst them at this time, says, "They paint Christ, the blessed Virgin, and other saints in black form; and devils and wicked men, white. Thus Christ and his apostles are black and Judas, white, while Michael is black, and the devil, white."

The bible really originates in Ancient Egypt, where the population, according to Herodotus and Aristotle, was black. Here the Jews received almost all of their early culture. Prof. Breasted, leading Egyptologist, says, "The ripe social and moral development of mankind in the Nile Valley which is 3000 years older than that of the Hebrews, contributed essentially to the formation of Hebrew literature. Our moral heritage therefore derives from a wider human past enormously older than the Hebrews, and it has come to us rather through the Hebrews than from them."

Psalms that read like those of the Bible were written by a Pharaoh, Amenophis IV, better known as Akhenaton, the Heretic King, 1300 B.C. or more than 400 years before David was born. Akhenaton, who was the father of Tut-Ankh-Amen, was extremely Negro in type. He was called "the most remarkable of the Pharaohs."

There were three African Popes of Rome: Victor (189-199 A.D.); Melchiades (311-312); and St. Gelasius (496 A.D.). It was Melchiades who led Christianity to final triumph against the Roman Empire.

On November 15, 218 B.C., Hannibal, a full-blooded Negro, marching through conquered territory in Spain and France, performed the astounding feat of crossing the Alps. With only 26,000 of his original force of 82,000 men remaining, he defeated Rome, the mightiest military power of that age, who had a million men, in every battle for the next fifteen years. Hannibal is the father of military strategy. His tactics are still taught in the leading military academies of the United States, England, France, Germany, and other lands.

The first slaves held in the United States were not black, but white. They were Europeans, mostly British, who died like flies on the slave-ships across. On one voyage 1,100 perished out of 1,500. At another time 250 out of 400. In Virginia, white servitude was for a limited period, but was sometimes extended for life. In the West Indies, particularly in the case of the Irish, it was for life. White people were sold in the United States up to 1826, fifty years after the signing of the Declaration of Independence. Andrew Johnson, President of the United States, was a runaway, and was advertised for in the newspapers.

The most ancient names for so-called black people are Nehesu, or Nubian; Ethiopian, and Moor from ancient Egypt, and Negro or Nigrita from West Africa. All the above are Native African words. "Negro" is probably the oldest as the Negritos are the oldest known branch of the human race. "Negro" comes from the River Niger. "Niger" found its way into Latin and since the people from that region were dark-skinned, Niger, nigra, nigrum came to mean black. Negro, Negrito, Nigrita, means "the people of the great river." Black and colored, like white, are, on the other hand, European words. Ethiopian and Moor were popularly used to describe the so-called blacks until 1500. Shakespeare uses "Negro" only once and uses it synonymously with Moor. Africa comes from the ancient Egyptian "Af-rui-ka," or Kafrica, the land of the Kaffir.

Haywood Shepherd, a free Negro, was the first person killed by John Brown's party of white and Negro raiders at Harper's Ferry in their efforts to free the slaves in 1859. Shepherd, while running off to arouse the white people, was shot dead in his tracks.

The blacks, like the whites, have been struggling for thousands of years to change their hair from its natural form. Negroes arranged their hair with hot irons in Egypt more than 5,000 years ago.

An American Negro has twenty chances to a white American's one of reaching a hundred years and over.

*Excerpted from "100 Amazing Facts About The Negro With Complete Proof" by J.A. Rogers, (New York: Helga M. Rogers, 1957, pp.4-15.

NOTES

Chapter I.

1. Napendo Ulinsi Milele, "Journey of the Songhai People", (Pennsylvania: Farme Press, 1987), p.51

2. Ibid., p. 44.

3 & 4. Ibid., p. 52.

5. Ibid., p. 47-48.

6. Ibid., p. 50.

7. J.A. Rogers, "Sex & Race: Vol. I", (New York: Helga M. Rogers, 1968), p. 265.

8. Ivan Van Sertima, "Black Women in Antiquity", (New Jersey: Transaction Publishers, 1988), p. 60. Reprinted by permission of Transaction Publishers.

9. Excerpt from "History of African Civilization" by E. Jefferson Murphy. Copyright © 1972 by E. Jefferson Murphy. Reprinted by permission of HarperCollins Publishers, Inc. p. 110-111.

10. Ibid., p. 119.

11. Ibid., p. 119.

12. Ibid., p. 120.

13. Ibid., p. 124.

Chapter IV

1. Reprinted with the permission of Scribner, an imprint of Simon & Schuster from "Two Nations: Black and White, Separate, Hostile, Unequal", by Andrew Hacker. Copyright © 1992 Andrew Hacker. p. 98.

2. J.A. Rogers, "Sex & Race: Vol III", (New York: Helga M. Rogers, 1989), p. 277.

3. Robert Froman, "Racism", (New York: Dell Publishing, 1972), p. 69.

4. Copyright ©1964 by The New York Times Company: Reprinted by permission.

5. From Newsweek, Mar. 29, 1993, p. 49. © 1993, Newsweek, Inc. All rights reserved. Reprinted by permission.

6. Reprinted by permission: Knight-Ridder Tribune News Service.

7. J. A. Rogers, "Sex & Race: Vol. III", (New York: Helga M. Rogers, 1989), p.146.

8. Ibid., p. 147.

9. Ibid., p. 148.

10. Robert Froman, "Racism", (New York: Dell Publishing, © 1972), p. 131.

Chapter V

1. Excerpt from History of African Civilization by E. Jefferson Murphy. Copyright © 1972 by E. Jefferson Murphy. Reprinted by permission of HarperCollins Publishers, Inc.

2. J.A. Rogers, "Sex & Race: Vol.II, (New York: Helga M. Rogers 1970) p. 355.

3. Ibid., p. 355.

4. Ibid., p. 355-356.

5. Ibid., p. 356

6. Dr. Clarence Walker, "Restoring The Queen Within: The Black Woman in Prophecy", (Audiotaped sermon, 1992).

7. "African Emporium" Boutique, (Wilmington, Delaware).

Chapter VI

1. Reprinted with the permission of Scribner, an imprint of Simon & Schuster
from Two Nations: Black And White, Separate, Hostile, Unequal by Andrew
Hacker. Copyright © 1992 Andrew Hacker. p.111.

2. Copyright © 1994 The Washington Post. Reprinted with permission.

3. Reprinted with the permission of Globe Communications Corporation, From
"Wonder Foods and Juices" by Carlson Wade and Dale Koppel, (Florida: Globe
Communications Corp., 1993), p. 23-47.

4. Ibid., p. 52, 53.

Chapter VII

1. Ivan Van Sertima, "Black Women in Antiquity", (New Jersey: Transaction Publishers, 1988), p.49. Reprinted by permission of Transaction Publishers.

2. Ibid., p. 49.

3. Ibid., p. 42.

4. Ibid., p. 57.

Bibliography

Alfred, C. _Art in Ancient Egypt._ London: Alec Tiranti, 1969.

Baldwin, Joseph H. _Psychology of Oppression._ New York: 1978.

ben-Jochanan, Yosef. _Africa, Mother of Western Civilization._ New York: Alkebu-Lan Books, 1970.

ben-Jochanan, Yosef. _African Origins of the Major "Western Religions."_ New York: Alkebu-Lan Books, 1970.

Billingsley, Andrew. _Black Families in White America._ Englewood Cliffs: Prentice-Hall, 1968.

Blyden, J.W. _Christianity, Islam, and the Negro Race._ Edinburgh University Press, 1967.

Bogle, Donald. _Toms, Coons, Mulattoes, Mammies, and Bucks: An Interpretive History of Blacks in American Film._ New York: Bantam, 1974.

Brownmiller, Susan. _Shirley Chisholm._ New York: Doubleday & Co., Inc., 1970.

Budge, E.A. Wallis _The Egyptian Book of the Dead: The Papyrus of Ani Egyptian Text Transliteration and Translation._ New York: Dover Publications, Inc., 1967.

Carwell, Hatti. _Blacks in Science: Astrophysicist to Zoologist._ New York: Exposition Press, 1977.

Citron, Abraham F. The _"Rightness of Whiteness": The World of the White Child in a Segregated Society._ Michigan: Michigan-Ohio Educational Laboratory, 1969.

Clegg, Legrand H. II. _Black Rulers of the Golden Age._ Journal of African Civilization. Vol. 4, No. 2, November, 1982.

Cripps, Thomas. _Slow Fade to Black: The Negro in American Film 1900-1942._ New York: Oxford, 1977.

Davis, George., Watson, Glegg. _Black Life in Corporate America._ New York: Anchor Press, Doubleday Book Co.

Diop, Cheikh Anta. _Origin of the Ancient Egyptians._ Journal of African Civilization, Vol. 4, No. 2, November 1982.

Essence Magazine, Vol. 21, Number 10, Feb. 1991.

Fazzini, R.A. _Art From the Age of Akhenaten._ Brooklyn, New York: Brooklyn, Museum Press, 1973.

Frenandez, Dr. John p. _Racism and Sexism in Corporate Life._ Mass: Lexington, Books.

Fon, Horsemann. *Black American Scholars: A Study of their Beginnings.* Michigan: Detroit Balamp Publishers.

Frankfort, Henri. *Ancient Egyptian Religions.* New York: Harper Torchbooks, 1961.

Freud, Sigmund. *Moses and Monotheism.* New York: Vintage Press, 1967.

Froman, Robert. *Racism.* New York: Dell Publishing Co., 1972.

Giddings, Paula. *When and Where I Enter: The Impact of Black Women on Race and Sex in America.* New York: Bantam Books, 1984.

Graves, Kersey. *The World's Sixteen Crucified Saviors: Or Christianity Before Christ.* New York: Truth Seeker Press, 1975.

Hacker, Andrew. *Two Nations, Black and White, Separate, Hostile, Unequal.* New York: Charles Scribner's Sons, 1992.

Hill, Robert B. *Informal Adoption Among Black Families.* New York: National Urban League, 1977.

Hill Robert B. *The Strengths of Black Families.* New York: National Urban League, 1971.

Hilliard, Dr. Asa. *Free Your Mind, Return to the Source: African Origins of Civilization.* (Lecture) Cocoa Beach, Florida: DEOMI, 1981.

Hodge, J.L., Struckmann, D.K. and Trost, L.D. *Cultural Bases of Racism and Group Oppression: An Examination of Traditional "Western" Concepts, Values and Institutional Structures Which Support Racism, Sexism and Elitism.* Berkeley: Two Riders Press, 1975.

Hurry, Jamieson B. *Imhotep: The Vizier and Physician of King Zoser and Afterwords the Egyptian God of Medicine.* Oxford University Press, 1928.

Jackson, John G. *Egypt and Christianity.* Journal of African Civilization, Vol. 4, No. 2, November, 1982.

James, George G.M. *Stolen Legacy.* San Francisco: Julian Richardson, 1976.

Jay, James M. *Negroes in Science: Natural Science Doctorates, 1876-1969.* Michigan: Detroit Balamp Publishers, 1971.

Jeffries, Leonard Jr. Civilization or Barbarism: The Legacy of Cheikh Anta Diop. Journal of African Civilization, Vol 4, No. 2, November, 1982.

Jones, Edward L. Black Zeus: African Mythology and History. Seattle: Edward L. Jones, Frayn Printing Co., 1972.

Jones, Edward L. Tutankhamen. Edward L. Jones and Associates: Washington, 1978.

Killens, John O. Explanation of the Black Psyche. New York: The New York Times, June 7, 1964.

Leab, Daniel J. *From Sambo to Superspade: The Black Experience in Motion Pictures.* Boston, Houghton-Mifflin, 1976.

Lerner, Gerda (Editor). *Black Women in White America.* New York: Vintage Press, 1973.

MacDonald, J. Fred. *Blacks and the White TV: Afro-Americans in Television Since 1948.* Chicago: Nelson-Hall Publishers, 1983.

Massey, Gerald. *A Book of the Beginnings: Containing an Attempt to Recover and Reconstitute the Lost Origins of the Myths and Mysteries, Types and Symbols, Religion and Language, with Egypt for the Mouthpiece and Africa as the Birthplace.* New Jersey: University Books, 1974.

Means, Sterling M. *Black Egypt and Her Negro Pharaohs.* Baltimore: Black Classics Press, 1978.

Means, Sterling M. *Ethiopia and the Missing Link in African History.* Pennsylvania: The Atlantis Publishing Co., 1980.

Meier, August., Rudwick, Elliott., Broderick, Francis L. (Editors). *Black Protest Thought in the Twentieth Century.* Macmillan Publishing Company, 1985.

Miele, Napendo Ulinzi. *The Journey of the Songhai People.* Pennsylvania: Farmer Press, 1987.

Mosley, William. *What Color Was Jesus?* Chicago: African American Images, 1987.

Murphy, E. Jefferson. *History of African Civilization.* New York: Dell Publishing, 1982.

Newell, V.K., Gipson, J.H., Rich, Waldo, L., & Stubblefield, B. (Editors). *Black Mathematicians and Their Works.* Pennsylvania: Dorrance & Co., 1980.

Obadele, I. and Obadele, A. *Civilization Before the Time of Christ.* New York: Dell, 1972.

Rodney, Walter. *How Europe Underdeveloped Africa.* Washington: Howard University Press, 1974.

Rogers, J.A. *Sex & Race, Vol. I.* New York: Helga M. Rogers, 1968.

Rogers, J.A. *Sex & Race, Vol. II.* New York: Helga M. Rogers, 1970.

Rogers, J.A. *Sex & Race, Vol. III.* New York: Helga M. Rogers, 1989.

Rogers, J.A. *100 Amazing Facts About the Negro With Complete Proof.* New York: Helga M. Rogers, 1957.

Rogers, J.A. *World's Great Men of Color.* New York: Macmillan Publishing Company, 1972.

Subira, George. *Black Folks Guide to Business Success.* New Jersey: Very Serious Business Enterprises, 1986.

Subira, George. *Black Folks Guide to Making Big Money in America.* New Jersey: Very Serious Business Enterprise.

The Philadelphia Inquirer. March 3, 1994.

The Philadelphia Inquirer. December 14, 1993

Van Sertima, Ivan. *Black Women in Antiquity.* New York: Transaction Publishers, 1988.

Wade, Carlson., Koppel, Dale. *Wonder Foods and Juices.* Florida: Globe Communications Corp., 1993.

Williams, Bruce. *The Lost Pharaohs of Nubia.* Journal of African Civilization. Vol. 4, No. 2, November, 1982.

Woodson, Carter G. *Miseducation of the Negro.* The Associated Publishers, 1969.

Wright, Richard. *Native Son.* New York: Harper-Collins Publications, Inc., 1989.

INDEX

INDEX

INDEX

INDEX